NEW CENTURY BIBLE COMMENTARY

General Editors

RONALD E. CLEMENTS   MATTHEW BLACK
(Old Testament)   (New Testament)

Lamentations

NEW CENTURY BIBLE COMMENTARY

Based on the Revised Standard Version

LAMENTATIONS

IAIN W. PROVAN

Lecturer in Hebrew and Old Testament Studies,
University of Edinburgh

Collins

MARSHALL PICKERING

WILLIAM B. EERDMANS, GRAND RAPIDS

7-10-91

First published in Great Britain in 1991 by Marshall Pickering
and in the USA by William B. Eerdmans Publishing Co.,
255 Jefferson Ave., S.E., Grand Rapids, Mich., 49503

Marshall Pickering is an imprint of
HarperCollinsReligious,
part of HarperCollins Publishers
77-85 Fulham Palace Road, London W6 8JB

Typeset by Medcalf Type Ltd, Bicester, Oxon
Printed in the United States of America

Marshall Pickering ISBN 0-551-02323-6
Eerdmans ISBN 0-8028-0547-7

For
Lynette

CONTENTS

PREFACE

This commentary was begun during my time as a Temporary Lecturer in Old Testament Studies at King's College, London, and completed during my time as a University of Wales Fellow attached to the Department of Religious Studies in the University College of North Wales in Bangor. I have many people to thank for help along the way. For the opportunity to write the commentary at all, I am indebted to the Old Testament editor of the series, Professor R. E. Clements. I have greatly valued his friendship and support throughout several uncertain years spent loitering with intent in the groves of Academe. Happily, I have been able to spend these years in two very agreeable environments; and my thanks must therefore go, secondly, to my academic friends and colleagues, together with the secretarial and library staff, in both London and Bangor. Their congeniality and helpfulness have made it a pleasure to work in both colleges. Particular thanks are due to the Revd R. J. Coggins (London) and Professor G. H. Jones (Bangor), who kindly agreed to read the manuscript and provided useful comments upon it; and to the Revd B. A. Mastin (Religious Studies), Dr R. Arnold (Animal Biology) and Mr G. Williams (Psychology), all from Bangor, for help with references, ostriches and computing facilities respectively. I was grateful for the periodic use of library facilities at Heythrop College, London; and for further bibliographical help from Dr D. G. Deboys, librarian of Tyndale House, Cambridge, and Dr G. I. Davies of the University of Cambridge. In spite of strenuous efforts, I was nevertheless unable to gain sight of the article by Treves which is mentioned in the Introduction; while Brandscheidt's new commentary on Lamentations came to my attention only after the manuscript was complete. Finally, I owe a debt of gratitude to my wife, Lynette, who has, as ever, been thoroughly supportive of my work, rarely complaining about the incursions into our family life and her own study time which it has often made. I could not have completed this commentary without her support; and it is to her that it is dedicated.

October 1989   Iain W. Provan

ABBREVIATIONS

BIBLICAL

OLD TESTAMENT (*OT*)

Gen.	Jg.	I Chr.	Ps.	Lam.	Ob.	Hag.
Exod.	Ru.	2 Chr.	Prov.	Ezek.	Jon.	Zech.
Lev.	I Sam.	Ezr.	Ec.	Dan.	Mic.	Mal.
Num.	2 Sam.	Neh.	Ca.	Hos.	Nah.	
Dt.	I Kg.	Est.	Isa.	Jl	Hab.	
Jos.	2 Kg.	Job	Jer.	Am.	Zeph.	

APOCRYPHA (*Apoc.*)

I Esd.	Tob.	Ad. Est.	Sir.	S. 3Ch.	Bel	I Mac.
2 Esd.	Jdt.	Wis.	Bar.	Sus.	Man.	2 Mac.
			E. Jer.			

NEW TESTAMENT (*NT*)

Mt.	Ac.	Gal.	I Th.	Tit.	I Pet.	3 Jn
Mk	Rom.	Eph.	2 Th.	Phm	2 Pet.	Jude
Lk.	I C.	Phil.	I Tim.	Heb.	I Jn	Rev.
Jn	2 C.	Col.	2 Tim.	Jas.	2 Jn	

GENERAL

AB	The Anchor Bible
AbrN	*Abr-Nahrain*
AET	Abhandlungen zur Evangelischen Theologie
AJ	Acta Jutlandica, Theology Series
Aq.	Aquila
ArOr	*Archiv Orientalni*
ASORSVS	American Schools of Oriental Research, Special Volume Series

ATD	Das Alte Testament Deutsch
AusBR	*Australian Biblical Review*
AV	*The Authorized Version*
BAT	Die Botschaft des Alten Testaments
B. Bat.	*Baba Batra*
BDB	F. Brown, S. R. Driver and C. A. Briggs (eds), *A Hebrew and English Lexicon of the Old Testament*
BEHE	Bibliothèque de L'école des Hautes Études, Section des Sciences Religieuses
BeO	*Bibbia e Oriente*
BH³	*Biblica Hebraica*, 3rd ed.
BHS	*Biblica Hebraica Stuttgartensia*
Bib	*Biblica*
BK	Biblischer Kommentar
BRen	*Bulletin Renan*
BSac	*Bibliotheca Sacra*
BZ	*Biblische Zeitschrift*
CB	Century Bible
CBSC	Cambridge Bible for Schools and Colleges
CBQ	*Catholic Biblical Quarterly*
CNEB	Cambridge Bible Commentary on the New English Bible
CTM	*Currents in Theology and Mission*
DAB	*Die Dichter des Alten Bundes*
DSB	Daily Study Bible
EchtB	Echter Bibel
FRLANT	Forschungen zur Religion und Literatur des Alten und Neuen Testaments
Gk.	Greek
GKC	E. Kautzsch (ed.), *Gesenius' Hebrew Grammar* (2nd English ed., revd by A. E. Cowley)
GSAT	Geistliche Schriftlesung, Altes Testament
HAT	Handbuch zum Alten Testament
Heb.	Hebrew
HKAT	Handkommentar zum Alten Testament
HS	Die Heilige Schrift des Alten Testaments (Bonn)

HSAT	Die Heilige Schrift des Alten Testaments (Tübingen)
HTR	*Harvard Theological Review*
IB	*The Interpreter's Bible*
ITC	International Theological Commentary
JB	*The Jerusalem Bible*
JBL	*Journal of Biblical Literature*
JNES	*Journal of Near Eastern Literature*
JQR	*Jewish Quarterly Review*
JR	*Journal of Religion*
JSS	*Journal of Semitic Studies*
KAT	Kommentar zum Alten Testament
KHC	Kurzer Hand-Commentar zum Alten Testament
LXX	The Septuagint
MT	The Massoretic Text
NEB	*The New English Bible*
NEchtB	Neue Echter Bibel
NIV	*The New International Version*
OL	The Old Latin
OLZ	*Orientalische Literaturzeitung*
Or	*Orientalia*
OTL	Old Testament Library
OTM	Old Testament Message, A Biblical-Theological Commentary
Proof	*Prooftexts: A Journal of Jewish Liturgy*
RB	*Revue Biblique*
RSV	*The Revised Standard Version*
SBT	Studies in Biblical Theology
SJOT	*Scandinavian Journal of the Old Testament*
STL	Studia Theologica Lundensia
Symm.	Symmachus
Syr.	The Peshitta
Ta'an.	*Ta'anit*
Targ.	The Targum
TB	The Torch Bible Commentaries
TTS	Trierer Theologische Studien
VT	*Vetus Testamentum*

Vulg.	The Vulgate
WMANT	Wissenschaftliche Monographien zum Alten und Neuen Testament
WS	Wuppertaller Studienbibel
WZKM	*Wiener Zeitschrift für die Kunde des Morgenlandes*
ZAW	*Zeitschrift für die alttestamentliche Wissenschaft*

SELECT BIBLIOGRAPHY

COMMENTARIES (*cited in the text by author only*)

Brandscheidt, R., *Das Buch der Klagelieder*, GSAT 10, Düsseldorf, 1988.

Budde, K., *Die Klagelieder*, in K. Budde *et al.*, *Die fünf Megillot*, KHC 17, Freiburg, Leipzig and Tübingen, 1898, pp. 70–108.

Davidson, R., *Jeremiah vol. 2, Lamentations*, DSB, Edinburgh and Philadelphia, 1985.

Ewald, H., *Die Psalmen und die Klagelieder*, DAB 1/2, 3rd ed., Göttingen, 1866.

Fuerst, W. J., *The Books of Ruth, Esther, Ecclesiastes, The Song of Songs, Lamentations*, CNEB, Cambridge, London, New York and Melbourne, 1975.

Gordis, R., *The Song of Songs and Lamentations*, 3rd ed., New York, 1974.

Gross, H., and J. Schreiner, *Klagelieder, Baruch*, NEchtB 14, Würzburg, 1986.

Haller, M., *Die Klagelieder*, in M. Haller and K. Galling, *Die fünf Megilloth*, HAT 1/18, Tübingen, 1940, pp. 91–113.

Hillers, D. R., *Lamentations*, AB 7A, Garden City, New York, 1972.

Kaiser, O., *Klagelieder*, in H. Ringgren *et al.*, *Sprüche, Prediger, Das Hohe Lied, Klagelieder, Das Buch Esther*, ATD 16, 3rd ed., Göttingen, 1981, pp. 291–386.

Knight, G. A. F., *Esther, Song of Songs, Lamentations*, TB, London, 1955.

Kodell, J., *Lamentations, Haggai, Zechariah, Malachi, Obadiah, Joel, Second Zechariah, Baruch*, OTM 14, Wilmington, Delaware, 1982.

Kraus, H.-J., *Klagelieder*, BK 20, 3rd ed., Neukirchen-Vluyn, 1968.

Lamparter, H., *Das Buch der Sehnsucht. Das Buch Ruth, Das Hohe Lied, Die Klagelieder*, BAT 16/2, Stuttgart, 1962.

Löhr, M., *Die Klagelieder des Jeremia*, HKAT 3/2/2, Göttingen, 1893.
Die Klagelieder, HSAT 2, 4th ed., Tübingen, 1923.

Martin-Achard, R., and S. P. Re'emi, *God's People in Crisis: A Commentary on the Book of Amos; A Commentary on the Book of*

Lamentations, ITC, Edinburgh and Grand Rapids, 1984.

Meek, T. J., and W. P. Merrill, *The Book of Lamentations*, *IB* 6, New York and Nashville, 1956, pp. 1–38.

Nötscher, F., *Die Klagelieder*, EchtB 2/2, Würzburg, 1947.

Paffrath, T., *Die Klagelieder*, HS 7/3, Bonn, 1932.

Peake, A. S., *Jeremiah vol. 2 and Lamentations*, CB, Edinburgh, 1911.

Plöger, O., *Die Klagelieder*, in E. Würthwein *et al.*, *Die fünf Megilloth*, HAT 1/18, 2nd ed., Tübingen, 1969, pp. 127–64.

Rudolph, W., *Die Klagelieder*, KAT 17/3, 2nd ed., Gütersloh, 1962.

Stoll, C-D., *Die Klagelieder*, WS, Wuppertal, 1986.

Streane, A. W., *Jeremiah, Lamentations*, CBSC, Cambridge, 1926.

Weiser, A., *Klagelieder*, in H. Ringgren and A. Weiser, *Das Hohe Lied, Klagelieder, Das Buch Esther*, ATD 16/2, Göttingen, 1958, pp. 39–112.

Wiesmann, H., *Die Klagelieder*, Frankfurt, 1954.

MONOGRAPHS AND ARTICLES (*cited in the text by author and short title*)

Albrektson, B., *Studies in the Text and Theology of the Book of Lamentations with a Critical Edition of the Peshitta Text*, STL 21, Lund, 1963.

Alexander, P. S., 'The Textual Tradition of Targum Lamentations', *AbrN* 24 (1986) 1–26.

Barton, J., *Oracles of God: Perceptions of Ancient Prophecy in Israel after the Exile* (London, 1986).

Bergler, S., 'Threni v – Nur ein alphabetisierendes Lied? Versuch einer Deutung', *VT* 27 (1977) 304–20.

Bickell, G., 'Kritische Bearbeitung der Klagelieder', *WZKM* 8 (1894) 101–21.

Brandscheidt, R., *Gotteszorn und Menschenleid: Die Gerichtsklage des leidenden Gerechten in Klgl 3*, TTS 41, Trier, 1983.

Brunet, G., *Les Lamentations contre Jérémie: Réinterprétation des quatre premières Lamentations*, BEHE 75, Paris, 1968.
'La cinquième Lamentation', *VT* 33 (1983) 149–70.

Budde, K., 'Das hebräische Klagelied', *ZAW* 2 (1882) 1–52.

Cannon, W. W., 'The Authorship of Lamentations', *BSac* 81 (1924) 42–58.

Cohen, S. J. D., 'The Destruction: From Scripture to Midrash', *Proof* 2 (1982) 18–39.

Cross, F. M., 'Studies in the Structure of Hebrew Verse: The Prosody of Lamentations 1:1–22', in C. L. Meyers and M. O'Connor (eds.), *The Word of the Lord Shall Go Forth: Essays in Honor of David Noel Freedman in Celebration of His Sixtieth Birthday*, ASORSVS 1, Winona Lake, Indiana, 1983, pp. 129–55.

Dahood, M., 'New Readings in Lamentations', *Bib* 59 (1978) 174–97.

Driver, G. R., 'Notes on the Text of Lamentations', *ZAW* 52 (1934) 308–9.

'Hebrew Notes on "Song of Songs" and "Lamentations" ', in W. Baumgartner *et al.* (eds.), *Festschrift für Alfred Bertholet*, Tübingen, 1950, pp. 134–46.

Ehrlich, A. B., *Randglossen zur hebräischen Bibel*, vol. 7, Leipzig, 1914.

Freedman, D. N., 'Acrostics and Metrics in Hebrew Poetry', *HTR* 65 (1972) 367–92.

'Acrostic Poems in the Hebrew Bible: Alphabetic and Otherwise', *CBQ* 48 (1986) 408–31.

Fries, S. A., 'Parallele zwischen den Klageliedern Cap. IV, V und der Maccabäerzeit', *ZAW* 13 (1893) 110–24.

Gottlieb, H., *A Study on the Text of Lamentations* AJ 48/12, Aarhus, 1978.

Gottwald, N. K., *Studies in the Book of Lamentations*, SBT 14, revd. ed., London, 1962.

Gunkel, H., 'Klagelieder Jeremiae' in H. Gunkel and L. Zscharnack (eds), *Die Religion in Geschichte und Gegenwart*, vol. 3, 2nd ed., Tübingen, 1929, cols. 1049–52.

Gwaltney, W. C., Jnr., 'The Biblical Book of Lamentations in the Context of Near Eastern Lament Literature', in W.W. Hallo, J.C. Moyer and L.G. Perdue (eds), *Scripture in Context II: More Essays on the Comparative Method*, Winona Lake, Indiana, 1983, pp. 191–211.

Hillers, D. R., 'History and Poetry in Lamentations', *CTM* 10 (1983) 155–61.

Johnson, B., 'Form and Message in Lamentations', *ZAW* 97 (1985) 58–73.

Kaiser, B. B., 'Poet as "Female Impersonator": The Image of Daughter Zion as Speaker in Biblical Poems of Suffering', *JR* 67 (1987) 164–82.

Lachs, S. T., 'The Date of Lamentations V', *JQR* 57 (1966–1967) 46–56.

Lanahan, W. F., 'The Speaking Voice in the Book of Lamentations', *JBL* 93 (1974) 41–9.

Levine, E., *The Aramaic Version of Lamentations*, New York, 1976.

Löhr, M., 'Der Sprachgebrauch des Buches der Klagelieder', *ZAW* 14 (1894) 31–50.

'Sind Thr. IV und V makkabäisch?', *ZAW* 14 (1894) 51–9.

'Threni III. und die jeremianische Autorschaft des Buches der Klagelieder', ZAW 24 (1904) 1–16.

McDaniel, T. F., 'Philological Studies in Lamentations', *Bib* 49 (1968) 27–53, 199–220.

'The Alleged Sumerian Influence upon Lamentations', *VT* 18 (1968) 198–209.

Mintz, A., 'The Rhetoric of Lamentations and the Representation of Catastrophe', *Proof* 2 (1982) 1-17.

Moore, M. S. 'Human Suffering in Lamentations', *RB* 90 (1983) 534–55.

Renkema, J., *'Misschien is er hoop . . . '. De theologische vooronderstellingen van het boek Klaagliederen*, Franeker, 1983.

Robinson, T. H., 'Notes on the Text of Lamentations', *ZAW* 51 (1933) 255–59.

Rudolph, W., 'Der Text der Klagelieder', *ZAW* 56 (1938) 101–22.

Segert, S., 'Zur literarischen Form und Funktion der fünf Megilloth (Im margine der neuesten Kommentare)', *ArOr* 33 (1965) 451–62.

Shea, W. H., 'The *qinah* Structure of the Book of Lamentations', *Bib* 60 (1979) 103–7.

Treves, M., 'Conjectures sur les dates et les sujets des Lamentations', *BRen* 95 (1963) 1–4.

Zenner, J. K., *Beiträge zur Erklärung der Klagelieder*, Freiburg, 1905.

INTRODUCTION

to

Lamentations

A. NAME AND PLACE IN THE CANON

In the Hebrew Bible, Lamentations has the title *'ēkāh*, 'How!', which is the first word of the book. Early Jewish tradition, however, knew the book as *qînôt*, 'Lamentations', and this tradition is reflected in both LXX and Vulg. Manuscripts and printed editions of the Versions frequently add 'of Jeremiah' or 'of Jeremiah the prophet' to this title.

The Scriptural status of Lamentations has never been a matter of dispute. The position in which it is placed in codices and printed editions of the Bible varies, however. The order found in the *English* Bibles used by Christians, in which Lamentations is closely associated with Jeremiah, derives from LXX, which was followed by Vulg. This reflects convictions about the authorship of the book (see 'Author, Date and Place of Composition' below). In manuscripts and editions of the *Hebrew* Bible, however, the listing reflects Jewish liturgical practice. Lamentations is associated with Ruth, Song of Songs, Ecclesiastes and Esther as one of the five scrolls (*Megilloth*) read in public worship at important festivals. The position of the *Megilloth* within the canon varies. They are most frequently to be found in the Writings, the third section of the Hebrew Bible, but they also appear between the Pentateuch and the Prophets, and are even found interspersed among the books of the Pentateuch (Barton, *Oracles*, 84). The order in which the five appear also varies, depending upon whether it is intended to reflect the order in which they were thought to have been composed (Ruth, Song of Songs, Ecclesiastes, Lamentations, Esther), or the order in which the Jewish festivals occurred at which they were read: Song of Songs (Passover), Ruth (Weeks), Lamentations (9th of Ab), Ecclesiastes (Tabernacles), Esther (Purim). The feast of the 9th of Ab, the fifth month of the Jewish calendar, commemorates, among other things, the destruction of both First and Second Temples, and is regarded by the Talmud (*Ta'an*. 30b) as equal in importance to the Day of Atonement.

The question as to which, if any, of these orders is 'original' is impossible to answer (Barton, *Oracles*, 82–91). The whole notion of a fixed 'canonical' order would have had no meaning in the period before codices came into use, and when all the scrolls containing the biblical writings were not universally available. Indeed, though we find different listings of the biblical books in various early external documents (cf., for example, *B. Bat.* 14b; Josephus, *Contra Apionem* 1:8; Jerome, 'Prologus galeatus', *Patrologia Latina*, 28, cols. 593–604), it is important to note that there is no suggestion here that any 'order' is the proper one or has special authority. Jerome, for example, himself includes Lamentations as part of Jeremiah, but notes that others include it among the Hagiographa. The search for an 'original' order is therefore a futile one.

B. LITERARY CHARACTER

Perhaps the most immediately noticeable feature of the poems in the book of Lamentations to the reader of the Hebrew text is their *alphabetic nature*. All the poems are alphabetic in one way or another, the number (22), and in most cases the sequence, of the letters in the Hebrew alphabet being a determinative factor in their composition. The fifth poem has twenty-two lines, while the first four are alphabetic acrostics. That is to say, the first stanza of each (or in the case of chapter 3, each line of the first stanza) begins with the first letter of the Hebrew alphabet (*ʾālep*), the second stanza (or each line of the second stanza) with the second letter (*bêt*), and so on. Interestingly, the order of the letters in chapter 1 of MT is slightly different to that in chapters 2–4. Chapter 1 has the usual order for the 16th and 17th letters (*ʿayin - pēh*), while chapters 2–4 have a less common order (*pēh - ʿayin*) which is also found in extra-biblical inscriptions (cf., for example, F. M. Cross, 'Newly found inscriptions in Old Canaanite and Early Phoenician scripts', *BASOR* 238 (1980) 1–20, on pp. 8–15), is reflected in the LXX of Prov. 31, and may have occurred originally in Ps. 34 (see the commentaries on these books). It seems that different traditions existed as to the order of the alphabet in biblical Hebrew and its precursors. Why the acrostic form was used by the author(s) of the first four Lamentations at all is not clear (cf. M. Löhr, 'Alphabetische und alphabetisierende Lieder im Alten Testament', *ZAW* 25 (1905) 173–98; R. Marcus, 'Alphabetic Acrostics in the Hellenistic and Roman Periods', *JNES* 6 (1947) 109–15; Gottwald, *Studies*, 23–32; and W. M. Soll, 'Babylonian and Biblical Acrostics', *Bib* 69 (1988) 305–23, for parallels and discussion), though it has most commonly been explained (e.g. by Gottwald, *Studies*, 28–32) as related to the message of the book in some way.

Another obvious feature of the poems, reflected in the traditional titles given to the book as a whole, is their character as *laments* or complaints. Much effort has gone into the attempt to classify them formally in a more specific way, though there is no consensus here. Gunkel, 'Klagelieder', for example, classified chapters 1, 2 and 4 as national funeral songs, chapter 3 as essentially an individual lament, and chapter 5 as a communal lament. Much subsequent discussion centred on whether chapter 3 was not better understood also as essentially a communal lament. More recently, Kraus, 8–13, has argued for the designation 'Lament over the ruined sanctuary' for the poems, noting parallels with Sumerian and Akkadian laments over ruined cities (cf. further Gwaltney, 'Book'); and Brandscheidt, *Gotteszorn und Menschenleid*, has classified chapters 1–2 and 4–5 as 'Complaint actualizing divine judgement' and chapter 3 as 'Legal complaint of the innocent sufferer'.

The main value of such debate is to make us aware of the many parallels which exist between the poems of Lamentations, on the one hand, and other laments found in the *OT* and Ancient Near Eastern texts generally, on the other. For when one is aware of the broader context of the poems, a third aspect of their literary character is apparent: that they are written to a very large extent in what may be described as *stereotypical language*. Expressions and motifs abound which were evidently part and parcel of a common fund of language upon which those lamenting in the Ancient Near East were accustomed to draw. Hillers, 'History and Poetry', notes, for example, the description of the ruined city in 5:18 and the references to cannibalism in 2:20, 4:10; and there are many more examples to which attention will be drawn in the commentary. Two further features of the language must also be noted. It is, on the one hand, largely metaphorical. The events which the poems describe are cloaked in non-literal language (e.g. the hunting language of 1:6) which renders the reality which lies behind them elusive. It is, on the other, demonstrably hyperbolic. For example, 1:3 tells us that Judah has gone into exile, a statement which stands in some tension with others in vv. 4, 11, 19–20 of the chapter (which suggest that some, if not many, people remained in Jerusalem). It is, further, a statement which, to our knowledge, exactly corresponds to reality at no point in Judah's history. That is, it was never true, not even in 587 B.C. (cf. P. R. Ackroyd, *Exile and Restoration*, London, 1968, 20–31), that Judah as an entity went into exile. 1:4, with its reference to the priests and maidens (at least in MT: see the commentary) who remain in the city being in mourning, is itself in tension with vv. 18–19, where the maidens have gone into captivity and the priests and elders have died; and v. 19 is further in tension, with regard to this last claim, with v. 6, if that verse is taken as saying that *all* the leaders of the community have gone into exile ('From the daughter of Zion has departed all her majesty': but see the commentary). V. 15, similarly, has the young men killed in battle, v. 18 has them carried off into exile. To point all this out is, of course, to be pedantic. It is, nevertheless, important to draw attention to the exaggeration which is apparent in the text, for reasons which will become clear below.

A fourth aspect of the literary character of Lamentations is that *more than one speaking voice* is to be found in the book. In chapter 1, for example, there are at least two: the anonymous speaker of the first half of the poem, and the speaker in its second half, who is Zion (see the commentary). Precisely how many speakers there are in the remainder of the book has been a matter of dispute. Wiesmann (132, 167, 209, 241–2, 271), for example, finds six in total: Zion (1:9c, 11c–15b, 16, 18–22; 2:11–12, 20–22; 3:48–51, 59–66; 4:3–6, 7–10); a narrator (1:1–6, 7–9b, 10–11b, 15c, 17; 2:1–10, 13–17; 4:1–2, 11–12; 5:11–14); the people (2:18–19; 3:34–38, 42–47; 4:17–20); Jeremiah (3:1–33, 39–41, 52–58; 4:13–16, 21–22); and two choirs (one in 5:1–5, 15–18, and the other in 5:6–10, 18–22). Lanahan, on the other hand, finds five: a reporter (1:1–11b, 15a, 17; 2:1–19); Zion (1:9c, 11c–22; 2:20–22); a defeated soldier (chapter 3); a bourgeois (chapter 4); and the community as a whole (chapter 5). I can find no evidence, however, for more than three: the main speaker (narrator), Zion, and the people of Zion. The narrator appears throughout the first four poems; Zion in chapters 1 and 2; and the people in chapters 4 and 5. The people or Zion—it is not clear which—also appear briefly in chapter 3. The first four poems, then, have something of the character of dialogues, and there are hints of differing perspectives between the voices who participate. Chapter 5, in contrast, is a monologue.

Fifthly, the question of the poetic metre of the poems has been much discussed. Unfortunately, there is nothing approaching a consensus on this matter (see Hillers, xxx–xxxvii, for a good brief discussion, and further Freedman, 'Acrostics and Metrics' and 'Acrostic Poems'). Whichever way we judge it, clearly chapter 5 is quite different metrically (as indeed it is in the degree to which it exhibits parallelism, cf. Hillers, xxxiii–xxxv) from chapters 1–4, in which the so-called *qînāh* metre first identified by Budde, 'Klagelied', predominates. We should not at present be on safe ground, however, if we were to venture further than this general observation.

As to their literary character, then, the poems in Lamentations are laments composed within an alphabetical framework, using language which is stereotypical, metaphorical and hyperbolic. In the first four, there is more than one speaker: the fifth is a monologue. The fifth poem is also different in structure and metre. Discussion as to the authorship, date and setting of the poems, their use and their theology, must take their character in these respects into account.

C. AUTHOR, DATE AND PLACE OF COMPOSITION

Ancient tradition, where it names an author for the book, is unanimous in ascribing it to the prophet Jeremiah. It has sometimes been argued (e.g. by Hillers, xix–xxi) that MT, which does not name the author, represents a different tradition, since it separates Lamentations from Jeremiah and places it in the Writings, thereby implying that Jeremiah was not the author. This is a curious argument. The Babylonian Talmud, after all, lists Lamentations among the Writings (*B. Bat.* 14b), but clearly still believes that Jeremiah wrote the book (*B. Bat.* 15a). There is no necessary connection between the placing of the book and a belief as to its authorship. Lamentations may have been included in the Writings, not because of any convictions about authorship, but simply because the way in which it was used as a liturgical text in the synagogue, along with the other *Megilloth*, differed for historical reasons from the way in which the Prophets were used (Barton, *Oracles*, 75–82). The fact that the Talmud does not list the five *Megilloth* together is irrelevant to the argument, since it gives merely a chronological listing of books within the Writings, and does not provide any clue as to why Lamentations happened to be listed there in the first place (Barton, *Oracles*, 86–88). MT cannot, then, be taken as reflecting a separate tradition. There is only one ancient tradition as to authorship of which we know, and it is reflected throughout the early Jewish-Christian documents. The LXX version of Lam. 1:1, which is followed closely by Vulg., begins as follows: 'And it came to pass after Israel had gone into captivity, and Jerusalem was laid waste, that Jeremiah sat weeping and composed this lament over Jerusalem and said . . .'. Such a view is also implicit in the juxtaposition of Lamentations and Jeremiah in LXX and in many other lists of the Old Testament books from this early period (see 'Name and Place in the Canon'). Targ. and Syr. both have headings which, like that of LXX, explicitly ascribe the book to Jeremiah; while in rabbinic writings, passages from Lamentations are frequently introduced with the words 'Jeremiah said'. This view of authorship, of course, carries with it implications about the date of the poems and their setting. They must all be dated within Jeremiah's lifetime, and must reflect settings with which he was familiar. LXX, for example, implies that they were written in Palestine shortly after the events of 587 B.C. Targ. for the most part also sets them against the background of 587, though occasionally citing other backgrounds for the individual text upon which it is commenting. The Targ. to 1:18–19 and 4:20, for example, refers to the death of King Josiah in 609 B.C. This is interesting in view of 2 Chr. 35:25, which may indicate that the Chronicler himself thought of Jeremiah and Lamentations in this context.

If it was the unanimous view of the ancients, so far as we can tell, that Jeremiah wrote Lamentations, this has certainly not been the consensus in the modern period. The traditional view has been defended by only a few scholars (e.g. Cannon, 'Authorship'; Wiesmann, 56–84), whose main emphasis has been upon the links which exist between the books of Jeremiah and Lamentations (e.g. Lam. 2:14/Jer. 5:31; 2:22/Jer. 6:25; 3:14/Jer. 20:7; 3:53/Jer. 38:6; 4:17/Jer. 2:36). Most have, however, argued that this view of authorship cannot be correct. Their reasons for adopting this position have varied, and by no means all the older arguments employed in defence of it have been widely accepted by more recent commentators. For example, general arguments from the acrostic structure of the first four poems, which has been characterized as unworthy of Jeremiah (e.g. Haller, 92); or from the vocabulary of the poems, which has close affinity with writings such as Ezekiel, Second Isaiah and Psalms as well as with Jeremiah (cf. Löhr, 'Sprachgebrauch'), do not find much recent support (cf., for example, Rudolph, 197; Hillers, xxii). Much more importance is attached to perceived inconsistencies between the picture of the author which may be constructed from Lamentations and the picture of the prophet which is found in the book of Jeremiah. Kraus, 13–15, for example, states that there are numerous passages in Lamentations which could not have come from the prophet. The fact that Jerusalem's misfortune is incomprehensible and unexpected; the emphasis on the splendour of Zion and the inviolability of the temple; the disappointment expressed over the failure of alliances; the emphasis on judgement on enemies and salvation for the people of God; and the particular stress on the guilt and fate of the priests and prophets of Jerusalem—all this indicates that the poems originated rather among the cult-prophets or priests of Jerusalem. Rudolph, 196–99, argues that 4:17–20 could not have been written by Jeremiah, since the author clearly hoped for help from the Egyptians (contrast Jer. 2:18, 37:5–10) and was one who fled from Jerusalem with Zedekiah (contrast Jer. 38:28–39:14); nor could chapter 3, since he never could have described his prophetic work as standing under God's anger (3:1, contrast Jer. 15:16, 17:16); nor chapter 5, since he did not stay in Palestine long enough after the catastrophe (Jer. 41–42) to have written 5:9 or 5:18. Hillers, xxi–xxii, adds that 4:20 is at variance with Jeremiah's blunt words to Zedekiah in Jer. 37:17; 1:10 is inconsistent with Jeremiah's prophecy of the destruction of the Temple (e.g. Jer. 26:4–6); and 2:9 is 'rather odd' in view of the fact that Jeremiah prophesied before, during and after the catastrophe (e.g. Jer. 42:7).

Most modern commentators, then, reject the idea that Jeremiah could have written the book. At best they are prepared only to concede that parts of the third poem have been put in Jeremiah's mouth as part of the strategy of its author (Rudolph, 227-45, cf. Löhr, 'Threni III'), or that this poem is dependent on Deuteronomistic reflection upon Jeremiah's prophetic role in the midst of a people suffering God's judgement (Brandscheidt, *Gotteszorn und Menschenleid*, 347–52). Authorship is spoken of among modern scholars for the most part no longer in terms of a named individual, but in terms of the circles from which the author(s) might have come. The majority understand the poems as originating among groups closely associated with the Temple (e.g. Kraus, 13–15; Albrektson, *Studies*, 219–30; Brunet, *Lamentations*, 114–25; G. Buccellati, 'Gli Israeliti di Palestina al tempo dell'esilio', *BeO* 2 (1960) 199–209). For many this makes little difference to their view of the date and setting of the poems. The majority of scholars would still argue that the book came into being, whether as one entity or by stages, in the Palestine of the period shortly after the events surrounding the fall of Jerusalem in 587 B.C. (e.g. Hillers, xviii–xix, xxiii). This is essentially also Rudolph's position (209–11), though he is somewhat unusual in that he dates the first poem shortly after 597 B.C. (cf. also Haller, 94, and Weiser, 43; S. B.

Gurewicz, 'The Problem of Lamentations 3', *AusBR* 8 (1960) 19–23, thinks that the third poem was written at this time). Proximity to the events is suggested to these scholars by such things as the style of the poems (the description of events is said to be 'fresh' or 'vivid') or their general tone (there is no trace of the kind of hope that appeared in later exilic times, that things would soon change for the better). Others, however, have argued for different settings (e.g. Egypt: Ewald, 321–26; Babylon: Löhr, 1893, xvii) and, more particularly, a diversity of dates for the individual poems. Kaiser, 300–2, for example, has recently dated chapter 2 in the middle of the fifth century; chapter 1 in the second half of that century; chapters 4 and 5 towards its end; and chapter 3 in the fourth century. Earlier scholars favoured second-century dates for various of these chapters. Fries, 'Parallele', placed chapters 4 and 5 here; Lachs, 'Date', chapter 5; and Treves, 'Conjectures', chapters 1 and 3–5.

How are these various arguments to be assessed? With regard to the setting in which the poems were written, it seems to me that virtually nothing can be said. They all concern events in Palestine, of course, but that does not mean that any was written there. There is simply no information in any of the poems which might help us on this point; and when Hillers, xxiii, states that 'In the absence of any strong evidence to the contrary . . . it seems best to suppose that the book was written in Palestine', the obvious question is 'Why?' Agnosticism seems a more appropriate response to the facts.

The matter of the date of the various poems is equally difficult. In the first place, it is not clear that, even if we were to accept the consensus view as to the historical events (i.e. the events surrounding the fall of the Judaean state in the early sixth century B.C.) to which they allude, we should be able to say very much about when they were *composed*. Historical allusions do not of themselves lead us to the date of composition of a text. Texts may look back on events from a variety of later standpoints; and all the arguments which have been employed in defining which particular standpoints were involved in this case seem entirely inconclusive.

There is, on the one hand, no way of telling whether the links with other *OT* material which exist are literary (Kaiser, 300–2) rather than simply traditional, and certainly no indication, if literary influence were to be granted, of the direction of that influence. It is clear on the other hand, first, that the 'freshness' and 'vividness' of a poem may have more to tell us about the creativity and imagination of the author than about when he lived; and secondly, that the lack of any explicit hope in the poems of Lamentations (to the extent that this is true: see the commentary on chapter 4) may be explicable in terms of the particular perspective of the author, or the specific use to which the book was intended to be put, rather than in terms of the general context in which it was written. To assume that all the individuals or groups of any given period shared the same outlook is an obvious error; and we know that these poems were in later times used liturgically on days of mourning, by people who could not generally be described as lacking a future hope. One thinks here, for example, of the use made of the Book of Lamentations by Jews in their services on the 9th of Ab, and by Christians in the *Tenebrae*, the Matins-Lauds services for the last three days of Holy Week. Mournful and hopeless songs have their place even in a generally optimistic, eschatologically-oriented community. It seems, then, that even if we felt sure about the historical background reflected by the poems, we would not have enough evidence to draw any conclusion as to a more specific date of composition.

Whether scholars are justified in feeling so confident about the historical background is, of course, itself open to question. The poems, after all, contain no dates or names which might help us in this respect. Everything depends upon deduction from the rather elusive language in which they are written. This is not such a simple task as many previous commentators seem to have imagined. If it is true (see 'Literary Character' above) that accounts of suffering in the Ancient Near East were to some extent, at least, written up in a stereotypical manner, without thought of the immediate 'facts', our first difficulty is to know when it is right to look for concrete historical reality behind the text at all. To take one example: are the 'friends' of Zion who are mentioned in the Lamentations 1 *historical* friends who might in principle be identified, as most commentators have assumed, or are they present simply because abandonment by friends is a traditional theme in laments (e.g. Ps. 38:11 [MT 38:12]), and this theme is expected here as a way of stressing a feeling of isolation? The answer is not obvious; and arguments about whether the friends are Edomites, Syrians or Judaeans therefore seem premature. Even if we feel it right to look for historical reality behind the text, we face further difficulty in the presence of metaphor and hyperbole in the text. Metaphorical language has a capacity for ambiguity, and it is not easy to pin it down, to be certain what the metaphors stand for in terms of historical events. For example, the 'precious things' mentioned in 1:10 might refer to temple treasure, as is usually assumed by commentators, but it might not (see the commentary). Hyperbolic language also makes the reconstruction of the historical reality which might have generated a poem difficult. For if it is the case that the language of a poem is frequently and demonstrably hyperbolic, how could we ever know *how much* inexactitude is actually present at any given point? How could we know which details could be used for historical reconstruction and which not? The nature of the language in the poems of Lamentations, then,—its stereotypical nature, the use of metaphor and hyperbole—is a limiting factor when we are searching for their historical background. Finally, there is the difficulty of tying such historical occurrences as we might feel we can with confidence extract from the text to *specific dates*. For many of the things apparently alluded to in our poems seem to have happened more than once. To take 1:10 again as an example, the allusion to illegal entry into the temple could be understood in relation to the events of 597, 587 or 167 B.C. (the attack on Jerusalem by Apollonius on the orders of Antiochus IV Epiphanes); and texts like I Kg. 14:25–28 and 2 Kg. 14:8–14 suggest that these are not the only possibilities.

Identifying the historical background of the poems is therefore not an easy matter. In chapter 2, the sixth and ninth verses, with their reference to the rejection and exile of the king, seem certainly to point to the events of 587 B.C. It might be thought that the third verse of chapter 1, with its 'Judah has gone into exile', must also indicate, in spite of the discussion above, one of the sixth century dates. In reality, however, this verse is of no help to us with regard to historical background. I have already noted that 'Judah' must be regarded as hyperbolic whichever background we read the poem against; and I should add here that several commentators on this verse have argued that 'exile' refers to voluntary migration rather than to forcible removal (see the commentary). The phrase might imply no more, then, than that a number of Judaeans fled in the face of the advancing enemy, or in the aftermath of the city's defeat. If scepticism still remains that exaggerated language of this type could have been used of much less significant events than those of the early 6th century, we should note 1 Mac. 1:38–40, which refer to the aftermath of the attack on Jerusalem by Apollonius in 167 B.C.E., and which read in *JB*'s translation as follows:

> The citizens of Jerusalem fled because of them, she became a
>   dwelling place of strangers;
> estranged from her own offspring, her children forsook her.
> Her sanctuary became as deserted as a wilderness, her feasts were
>   turned into mourning,
> her sabbaths into a mockery, her honour into reproach.
> Her dishonour now fully matched her former glory, her greatness
>   was turned into grief.

1:53 adds that in the circumstances, Israel was forced '. . . into hiding in all their places of refuge'. There was, of course, no depopulation of Jerusalem of the proportions of 597 or 587 B.C.E. in 167 B.C.E. The reader of these verses in 1 Mac. 1 would, however, be forgiven for thinking that there must have been; and the warning is apparent for all readers of Lamentations 1. Clearly, if the author of I Maccabees could have written in such a way of the events of 167 B.C., we cannot insist that the author of Lam. 1:3 must have been thinking of events in the sixth century. The historical background of chapter 1, then, is unclear, and the same must be said of chapter 4, where similar considerations apply (cf. 4:14–16, 22), and chapters 3 and 5, where there is even less to go on than in chapter 1.

There does not seem to be, then, any evidence with regard to date or place of composition which would help us either to confirm or deny Jeremianic authorship of the poems of Lamentations. Such evidence as exists is consistent with a variety of positions. Can the question of authorship be resolved on its own terms? It does not seem to me that it can. The evidence with regard to whether the poems were written by one person or more is, first of all, inconclusive. On the one hand, similar structure, language and themes do not prove (*contra* Rudolph, 193–95, among others) common authorship. The extent to which the poems are similar to each other could be the result of different authors drawing on common traditions, or even of the deliberate modelling of later poems on earlier ones. The only explicit evidence of a *literary* connection between poems in the book is that found in 3:1 (see the introduction to chapter 3), and this could be explained either in terms of common authorship or in terms of the author of chapter 3 building on the earlier chapter 2. The latter is the position adopted, for example, by Brandscheidt, *Gotteszorn und Menschenleid*, 204–231, who is the latest in a long line of scholars to argue on the basis of *differences* between the poems that they were *not* written by one author. Chapter 2, she argues, is different from chapter 1 in that the former understands judgment as signifying the end of the election of Israel and the latter does not. Chapter 3 differs from chapter 2 in orthography; in the use which is made of the same images (2:3–4 compared with 3:3; 2:16a compared with 3:46); and in the more positive note which it strikes. Chapter 5 differs from all the others, since it is a non-acrostic community lament. Unlike chapter 4, it is not certain of divine intervention. In Brandscheidt's view, chapter 2 was written first, closely followed by chapter 1 and then chapter 5. All these poems were used first in public worship. The author of chapters 3 and 4, which are similar in structure, style and message, and are more interested than the others in the fate of the individual than that of the community as a whole, later combined all five poems in one book.

Brandscheidt's case, however, like that of those who preceded her in arguing in such a way, cannot be sustained; for the differences which she notes could equally well be explained (and have been explained by other scholars) in terms of a single author. Orthographic variation and varying use of similar imagery are frequently to be found in works written by one author; while the different perspectives of the various poems could be accounted for in terms of the overall purpose of such an author. Brandscheidt herself, after all, shows how they all contribute to the overall purpose of one person, whom she prefers to think of as an editor. Even the very different form of chapter 5 could be explained in such a way. Bergler, 'Threni v', for example, has argued that this chapter is deliberately structured as it is so as to communicate a hidden message, which appears when the initial letters of each verse (except in vv. 17–18) are joined together. More plausibly, scholars like Johnson and Lanahan have sought to explain chapter 5 in terms of the progression of thought within the book. Johnson, 'Form', argues that the alphabetical form of the five laments is a means of emphasizing their theological message. The message of each of the first four (acrostic) songs hinges on a turning point half-way through, the message of the book being found in chapter 3, the half-way point of the book, where the acrostic structure of the book intensifies. The central section of this chapter, which is also the central section of the book, provides the answer to the problem with which the book wrestles; while the non-acrostic chapter 5 functions well as the book's conclusion, since it contains the prayer for forgiveness which the first four chapters demand. Lanahan, 'Voice', 45, 49, thinks that the acrostic form signifies inexorable certitude about the total fulfilment of God's punitive will, from (as we would say) A to Z. By chapter 5, the fund of torments has been exhausted: there remains no possible suffering which has not already been endured. The disappearance of the acrostic structure corresponds to the shrinking back from a feeling of inevitability which is expressed in the communal prayer to God. For an analysis of chapter 5 which is similar in style to these, see the introduction to that chapter below. The only difference between the poems which is at all difficult to account for in terms of authorial purpose is that between the order of the alphabet in chapter 1 when compared with chapters 2–4 (see 'Literary Character' above). However, we simply do not know enough about the literary conventions governing this matter to decide whether one author could have followed two different patterns.

Taken as a whole, then, the evidence is insufficient for any conclusion to be drawn as to whether Lamentations was written by one author or many. The same may be said in regard to the question as to whether a putative single author might have been Jeremiah. On the one hand, the fact that the book of Lamentations has language and themes in common with the book of Jeremiah does not prove that Jeremiah wrote it. The existence of common language and themes could rather be understood in terms of dependence by the author(s) of our poems on the Jeremianic tradition. On the other hand, the differences which have been detected between the books do not compel us to believe that Jeremiah did *not* write Lamentations. Even if their literary character permitted us in principle to draw conclusions for authorship from these differences, many of the individual arguments advanced would not stand up to close inspection. There *is* talk both of the guilt of the priests and prophets of Jerusalem and of judgment on enemies/salvation for the people of God in the book of Jeremiah. 4:18–19 is not necessarily to be taken literally of flight from Jerusalem, nor 5:18 literally of an uninhabited Zion. An expression of moral outrage at foreign violation of the sanctuary (1:10) is not a claim that the sanctuary is inviolable, and is certainly not inconsistent with a claim that God is the prime mover in the event; and a claim that prophets in general have ceased speaking (2:9), if that is what it is, does not imply that all prophets have done so (see the commentary on all these points). In fact, however, it is by no means clear, given the literary character of the books of Lamentations and Jeremiah, that any such conclusions *can* be drawn from this kind of comparison.

In the first place, the extent to which a picture of the putative *author* of Lamentations may be reconstructed from the poems is questionable. It is generally assumed by scholars that the individual statements of the poems may be taken as reflecting this author's own perspective and life-experience. These statements are, however, uttered by more than one voice, and the voices utter words from more than one perspective (see 'Literary Character' above). It is never made clear in the book whether the author is actually to be identified with *any* of the speakers, much less *which* of the voices might be his. We are on very shaky ground, then, if we insist that 4:17–20, for example, must reflect the author's point of view. Even the overall perspective of the book which includes all these other perspectives (see 'Theology' below) may not correspond to that of the author himself, but may only be the perspective of the community whom the characters of the book represent. That is to say, the author might be intent upon portraying the dilemma in which the community finds itself, caught between faith and doubt, rather than indicating that this is his own position. If, for the sake of argument, however, we allow that this overall view of the book is also the view of the author, is it such that it could not have been that of Jeremiah? Do we know enough about Jeremiah and his activity after the fall of Jerusalem to be able to say?

We cannot claim that we do. The only account which we possess of this period in Jeremiah's life is found in Jer. 39–44; and though it often seems to have been forgotten in discussion about the authorship of Lamentations, the picture of Jeremiah which we find here, as in the rest of the book, cannot be taken as equivalent to that of the 'real' Jeremiah. It is a picture, on the contrary, which, like the pictures of Jesus in the Gospels, serves particular theological ends (cf., for example, E. W. Nicholson, *Preaching to the Exiles: A Study of the Prose Tradition in the Book of Jeremiah*, Oxford, 1970; W. Thiel, *Die deuteronomistische Redaktion von Jeremia 26–45*, WMANT 52, Neukirchen-Vluyn, 1981); and as there is much dispute about what the 'historical' Jesus who lies behind the Gospel pictures actually said and did, so there is much dispute about the 'Life of Jeremiah'. No simple connection can be made between 'what

Jeremiah said and did' and 'what the book of Jeremiah claims Jeremiah said and did' (cf. R. P. Carroll, *Jeremiah*, OTL, London, 1986, pp. 55–64). There are inherent dangers, then, in referring to Jer. 39–44 in any discussion about the likelihood that Jeremiah did or did not compose Lamentations. We cannot simply assume that conflict between *pictures* of Jeremiah and the author of Lamentations necessarily implies that the historical Jeremiah could not have written the latter book. Even if Jer. 39–44 were to be read as if it were what we might call 'straightforward history', it would in any case settle very little. Granted, the oracle of chapter 42 is more positive in tone than is the book of Lamentations taken as a whole. One could well argue, however, if one were so minded, that this tells us nothing about Jeremiah's state of mind between the destruction of the city (chapter 39) and the date of that oracle, nor indeed afterwards; and one could go on to provide imaginative explanations as to why Jeremiah might have been torn with doubt before and after this time, citing other passages (e.g. Jer. 20:7–18) which could be argued to indicate that his personality was such that he was prone to this sort of mental turmoil. However we regard the evidence of the book of Jeremiah, then, it seems inconclusive.

The general conclusion to which we are forced at the end of this section, then, is that we simply have insufficient evidence, when the literary character of the poems in Lamentations is taken into account, to decide questions of authorship and place of composition. The second poem, and therefore the book as a whole, may, with a degree of certainty, be dated between the 6th and the 2nd centuries B.C.; but beyond this we may not go.

D. PRIVATE OR PUBLIC USE?

Among Jews of the Talmudic period, the book of Lamentations was apparently read only in private (*Ta'an.* 30a). Subsequently, however, it came to be used liturgically at public gatherings by both Jews and Christians (e.g by Jews in their services on the 9th of Ab, and by Christians in the *Tenebrae*, the Matins-Lauds services for the last three days of Holy Week). When scholars have asked themselves which of these settings is likely to have been the one which the author(s) of the poems had in mind as they were being written, they have usually favoured the latter, noting, among other things, the alternation among speakers in some of the poems; *OT* evidence for public mourning over Jerusalem (cf. Jer. 41:4–5 and Zech. 7:2–7); and Ancient Near Eastern parallels for such public lamenting. The precise significance of these parallels is disputed (cf. McDaniel, 'Influence'; Weiser, 40–42), and few would be so specific as Gwaltney, 'Book', who thinks that returning exiles familiar with Mesopotamian liturgies for rebuilding demolished shrines wrote or edited the five poems of Lamentations for use in bewailing the fallen sanctuary as the clearing of the site began in preparation for reconstruction. That the poems were originally designed for cultic use of some kind would, however, generally be accepted.

As with questions of date, authorship and place of composition, however, the evidence does not seem sufficient for any decision to be taken as to originally intended use. The first four poems do lend themselves to recitation by different speakers, but the presence of different voices may also be understood as a literary device, the intention being to introduce differing perspectives. They may have been used in public worship of the type described in Jeremiah and Zechariah and paralleled in other parts of the Ancient Near East, but the alternation in voices does not compel us to believe that this was so. If it cannot positively be argued, then, that the structure of the poems favours an originally private use (cf., for example, Segert, 'Form', who argues along these lines with regard to the acrostic structure of chapter 3), it cannot be argued either that it favours public use. We are completely in the dark so far as this question is concerned.

E. THEOLOGY

That the poems in Lamentations contain theological ideas is self-evident. The suffering which is being endured by the people, for example, is explained as a result of sin (e.g. 1:5, 2:14, 3:42, 4:13,

5:16) and in terms of God's anger (e.g. 1:12, 2:1, 3:1, 4:11, 5:22); and hope for the future is grounded in God's just (1:21–22) and merciful (3:21–33) nature. There has been some disagreement, however, as to how, if at all, the various ideas may be drawn together to give a unified theological perspective. Does the book of Lamentations have 'a theology' at all?

Three major monographs which have appeared since the war have been devoted entirely or in substantial degree to the theology of the book. Gottwald, *Studies*, 47–62, has argued that Lamentations, like Job, deals with the problem of suffering, though on a national scale. The key to the book's theology lies in the tension between the historical reality of national catastrophe and the Deuteronomic faith in a doctrine of retribution and reward. Why should righteous Israel suffer so great a reversal after her earnest attempts at reform under King Josiah (cf. 2 Kg. 22–23)? Lamentations does not resolve this question, and, though it clearly expresses hope for the future, it thus foreshadows Wisdom literature like Job in pointing finally to the mystery of the divine ways. Albrektson, *Studies*, 214–39, agrees that tension is apparent in the book; but it is tension between the historical reality of the disaster and specific concepts like the inviolability of Jerusalem. As links with both the cult-traditions of Jerusalem and Deuteronomic traditions show, the author(s) of Lamentations sought to explain the failure of Zion theology in terms of Deuteronomic theology, and to lead Israel back to faith in a person rather than a place. The Deuteronomic view of the catastrophe as a divine judgment is the 'solution' to the problem created by the tension between faith and historical reality. Renkema, *Misschien is er hoop*, thinks that the authors of Lamentations accepted that the catastrophe was judgment for sin, and indeed, very great sin, if the severity of the punishment was to be taken as an indicator. They were, however, still uncertain about the true nature of their guilt: they could not believe that their sins were those indicated by the prophets. They therefore struggled with unresolved questions, unable to move beyond the paradox that, though they had abandoned all hope in God, yet they had no choice but to continue to express hope in him.

All three monographs have weaknesses. Gottwald's case is the weakest of all, since the text again and again explicitly states that Israel suffers because of sin (e.g. 1:5, 2:14, 3:42, 4:13, 5:16). Sufficient account does not seem to be taken of this material in his analysis of the book as a whole. Nor is it clear, *contra* Albrektson, that there *is* any 'resolution' of the 'problems' of the book within the book itself, in terms of the dominance of one perspective over others (cf. Moore, 'Suffering'). Although deuteronomic and Zion traditions are clearly reflected in the book, the text seems much more equivocal than Albrektson implies; and his emphasis on the hopeful nature of the book, something which Gottwald also stresses, seems particularly misguided. That there are statements of faith and hope in the book is, of course, not to be disputed. Chapter 4 ends with a clear note of hope, and chapter 3 has its moments (3:21–33). The latter chapter as a whole has often been characterised as the high point of the book, structurally speaking: it is here, that the 'real' message of the book, the message of hope, is to be found. Both Johnson, 'Form', and Brandscheidt, (*Gotteszorn und Menschenleid*) have recently argued in this way, the latter claiming (pp. 20–235, 344–52) that chapter 3 is the *Glaubensdichtung* ('poem of faith') of a righteous individual coming to terms with the judgment upon the community in which he has been caught up. The extent to which chapter 3 may be described as a poem of faith, however, much less the book as a whole as a document of faith, is open to question. For chapter 3 is in reality a mixture of hope and despair, and it ends in a plea to God which leaves us balanced on a knife-edge between these two (see the commentary). The reader who reads the chapter to the end does not receive an impression of great hopefulness. Nor is the reader who reads the *book* to the end left with this impression of the book as a whole. Lamentations does not, after all, end with 3:21–27, but with 5:22; and in spite of many valiant attempts to interpret this verse in a hopeful manner (e.g. Streane, 364, who states that '. . . the Book does in fact close with the language of hope . . .', whilst conceding that this is not '. . . apparent on the first reading . . .'!), it cannot plausibly be done. After many struggles, it is doubt, not hope, with which the book leaves us; and to characterise Lamentations as a hopeful book is therefore to mislead.

Although Renkema in turn, then, does not appear to be correct in his assertion that there is any uncertainty as to the true nature of the people's guilt in the book, in his general emphasis upon the juxtaposition of faith and doubt he is much nearer the mark in his description of the theology of Lamentations than either Gottwald or Albrektson. The first four poems, as the commentary shows, contain debate as well as lament, differing perspectives being offered upon the suffering which is being endured. The 'orthodox' view of suffering is present throughout the book: suffering is the punishment of God for sin, and the correct response to it is humble acceptance of the situation and repentance, trusting in God's love (e.g. 1:8–9; 3:21–27, 40–42). Even the narrator, however, in whose contributions this view is most consistently adhered to, is in a turmoil of doubt (chapter 3); while in the speeches of Zion and her people, questions are raised, explicitly or implicitly, which are far-reaching. There is doubt as to God's even-handedness in the administration of justice and as to the appropriateness of the punishment with regard to the crime (1:22; 2:20); as to the extent to which he is even in control of the situation (3:34–36); and as to whether hope for the future is misplaced (5:22). While there is apparently acknowledgment of sin, it does not seem so wholehearted as in the speeches of the narrator, being accompanied by reproach of God for his actions (2:20–22; 5:2–3, 5). The contribution of the people in the fifth poem, indeed, illustrates the tenor of these speeches well. In contrast to other community laments in the *OT*, Lamentations 5 is mainly taken up with lament over the people's misery (vv. 1–18), only a very brief space being given to petition (vv. 19–22). In the lament, reproach (vv. 2–3, 5) plays a greater role than confession of sin (v. 16); while in the petition, doubt is much more evident than faith. This does not suggest a hopeful people, and does not even imply a repentant one. The 'orthodox' view in the end does not prevail. To the extent that such a diversity of viewpoints can be described as 'a theology' at all, then—and we must be careful, as Moore ('Suffering', 538) has pointed out, not to oversimplify—, the theology of Lamentations is, as Renkema has put it, 'a theology ending in a question mark'.

This is not a theology which is bound to one disaster. Whatever its historical background, the book could, like the book of Job, be read against the background of any disaster, and has indeed been so read historically. Early Christians (e.g. Justin Martyr, *First Apology*, 72) often interpreted it in the light of Christ's Passion, for example; while Jews read it in the light of the destruction of Jerusalem in 70 A.D. (Targ. to 1:19) and, more generally, as setting forth the eternal paradigm of Jewish suffering (*Lamentations Rabbati*, a rabbinic commentary of the fifth to the seventh centuries A.D.). Cohen, 'Destruction', has, indeed, argued that the lack of any evidence that the author of Lamentations felt it important to give us specific information about date and background is an indication that he himself was not so much interested in the significance of particular historical events as he was concerned to portray an aspect of general human experience. He '. . . may have been attempting to confront catastrophe as an absolute', lamenting not only the fall of Jerusalem, '. . . but also all falls from divine grace, all disasters inflicted upon a sinful humanity'. Whether this is correct or not, clearly it is only in the sense that Lamentations is generally 'a book about suffering' that it can have contemporary meaning for the modern critical reader. In its questioning it is, indeed, a very modern book. The key to its contemporary handling lies in the recognition that we are being drawn by it into the debate which it presents to us. We are being invited, along with the other onlookers described in the text (e.g. at 1:12), to empathise with the suffering people of the poems, to feel the sense of isolation and abandonment, frustration and anger, which suffering often brings. We are further being invited to learn from their experience, to participate in their attempt to relate their experience to the reality of God. The book reminds us in a forceful way of the challenge of suffering to faith, and invites us to feel and to ponder its significance. Like so much else in the *OT*, then, it provokes questions rather than providing answers. The 'correct' resolution of 'the problem of suffering' is not given to us in the book. As Mintz,

'Rhetoric', 17, has put it so well, lamentation expresses only '. . . man's struggle to speak in the face of God's silence'. The only answers which can be given to the questions raised by the 'voices' of the book must be given, as Lanahan's analysis ('Voice', 49) implies, by the voice which is not itself heard in the book: the voice of God himself.

F. TEXT AND INTERPRETATION

The assumption of all modern commentators on Lamentations has been that their task is to write a commentary on the original Hebrew text, or a text as close to the original as we can possibly get, rather than simply on one of the Hebrew texts or translations of a Hebrew text of the book which we actually possess. All modern commentaries on Lamentations are therefore commentaries upon a Hebrew text which does not actually exist in reality, but which has been created to a greater or lesser degree by mixing readings from a main Hebrew text (e.g. the Leningrad Codex, used in the most recent work) with readings derived either from other Hebrew texts or from the Versions (e.g. LXX, Syr., Targ.). The extent to which such mixing takes place depends upon the individual commentator's views on a number of issues. The importance which (s)he attaches to irregularities in metre or grammar and syntax as a sign of textual corruption; the degree to which (s)he believes it is possible to work back to the hypothetical *Vorlage* of any given Version; the extent to which (s)he believes that the comparison of different readings makes possible a decision as to which is 'better'— these are some of the things which will influence a scholar's opinions with regard to the question of 'original text'. It might be of some help for the reader of this commentary, and it will certainly remove the necessity for endless repetition later on, if I give here a (necessarily) brief outline of where I stand in general on such issues.

In the first place, I am not at all convinced that we know nearly enough about the conventions governing ancient Hebrew poetry to be able to draw any conclusion in terms of the originality of a text from variation in metre and line-length. Recent commentators have in any case refused to go so far along this path as some earlier scholars (e.g. Bickell, 'Bearbeitung'); and in my view still more caution is required (cf. Freedman, 'Acrostics and Metrics'). Nor is it clear to me, for similar reasons, that unusual grammar or syntax necessarily implies that a text is corrupt. Our 'rules' of Hebrew grammar are, after all, approximations which are always subject in principle to readjustment on the basis of the empirical study of texts. A possible response to any given 'corrupt' text is the readjustment of our system to accommodate it. They are, moreover, *modern* approximations, with which we cannot know that the ancient Israelites would have been familiar. It is certainly arguable that the Massoretic scribes, themselves at some distance from the time of composition but considerably closer than we are, would not have recognised our rules. They were clearly prepared to suggest alternative readings where the consonantal text was problematic for them, in order that the text could be read; yet they seem to have found many fewer difficult readings than have modern scholars. Finally, even if our 'rules' were also the rules operating in Israelite society in general, this does not mean that they were always consistently applied by everyone, any more than the 'rules' of English grammar and syntax are always so applied by everyone who speaks English. For all these reasons, a conservative approach to ancient Hebrew texts is required; and such an approach is adopted in this commentary. Little discussion is therefore devoted to the many emendations made by scholars to the text which we may describe as 'speculative', i.e. lacking any support from the Versions, since it does not seem to me much of an advance to replace a difficult text which is attested with a readily comprehensible one which is not. The only exceptions to this general rule are emendations which have been suggested since the publication of the last two major commentaries on Lamentations in English (Hillers, in 1972; and Gordis, in 1974); or emendations which lie behind the translations offered by *RSV*, *JB*, *NEB* and *NIV*. Mention is made of the latter by way of explanation of these versions, which are referred to in the commentary as useful illustrative material in terms both of text and of interpretation. The former are noted merely for the sake of scholarly completeness.

Where the various 'witnesses' to the text disagree, of course, the situation is quite different; for in this case there is at least possible attestation of differences between Hebrew texts. I say 'possible', because one cannot assume, of course, that apparent differences between, say, MT and LXX necessarily signify that LXX was dependent upon a different Hebrew *Vorlage*. Every translation is also in part an interpretation; and in every copying of a translation there is the possibility of internal textual corruption. One need only compare Albrektson's assessment (*Studies*) of the Versional evidence in Lamentations with that of T. H. Robinson in *BH³* to see the very wide range of possibilities which are open to us in explaining the relationship of the Versions to the Hebrew. Still, the possibility remains. In this case, and in the case where actually extant Hebrew texts disagree, the question of originality presses itself upon us. But how is a choice to be made between different readings?

Textual critics have often written as if interpretative abilities play no part in such decisions; as if the application of a set of 'scientific' rules could solve such problems in an objective manner. This is clearly not so. For paramount in the actual practice of textual criticism have always been judgments about the sense which particular readings make in the context. In most cases, after all, a comparison of two readings cannot of itself tell us which might have preceded the other. It might be reasonably clear that confusion of similar letters, transposition of letters, errors of joining and dividing words, haplography/dittography, homoioteleuton or homoioarcton has taken place. With the exception of homoioteleuton or homoioarcton, however, where explanations in terms of omission in the course of copying from text A to text B are intrinsically more probable than explanations in terms of deliberate or accidental insertion in the course of copying from B to A, decisions about the *direction* of the corruption depend almost entirely upon judgments about which reading makes the better sense. It is precisely because of the priority of sense that the famous rule of *lectio difficilior* (the more difficult reading of two is probably the older, since it is more likely that this was transformed into the easier of the two than vice versa) has been more honoured by commentators in the breach than in the observance, often being cited only after all other arguments have been exhausted. For scholars have in general preferred to believe that the original text made better, not worse, sense than later versions of it. This assumption seems at least as reasonable as its opposite; and it is the working assumption which lies behind most of the textual decisions taken in the present commentary. The reasoning behind such decisions will not, however, always be given in the commentary, since to do this would make it impossibly long and tedious. In general, I shall discuss Hebrew readings implied by the Versions which I judge inferior in sense only where they have previously been accepted as original by other scholars, or where they lie behind the translations of *RSV, JB, NEB* and *NIV*. Where it seems impossible to decide between different readings as to which is better, I shall discuss the various possibilities, but leave the matter unresolved, since there seems no good reason in these cases why one text (e.g. MT) should *apriori* be given precedence over another. I shall generally not discuss differences between MT and the Versions which I do not judge to be significant in terms of sense.

It should be quite clear to the reader by now that a commentary on a biblical text, indeed on any text, is a highly personal piece of work. This is not only true at the level of text, in deciding which text to comment upon; it is also true (to the extent to which these two levels may be distinguished) at the level of interpretation, in deciding what the accepted text is likely to mean. Texts are slippery items, poetic texts particularly so; and to them every reader brings his or her own assumptions and questions, which may or may not be shared by others. All that one can hope to do as a commentator, in order to be as efficient a bridge between the text and the reader as possible, is to attempt to indicate the possibilities of interpretation which occur to him in reading the text, offering some indication as to which, if any, he feels is more satisfactory than the rest. I have attempted, therefore, to be as indecisive as possible where matters of interpretation are concerned, in the hope that the reader will thereby be driven to engage with the text rather than simply with the commentary. For commentaries should not be read as if they contained 'the meaning' of the text, but rather as a catalyst for the reader's own imaginative interaction with it. I have, however, made two general decisions about the interpretation of the poems of which the reader should be aware.

I have, in the first place, refrained from including in the commentary any reference to the possible historical events which might have been in the author's mind as he wrote. In part, this is because I am generally sceptical about our ability to know this (see 'Literary Character' and 'Author, Date and Place of Composition'). To a much greater extent, however, it is because, although it is interesting to speculate about such matters, our reading of the text in a meaningful way for the present (see 'Theology' above) does not depend upon knowing its specific historical background. The biblical texts have retained a lasting value for their readers precisely because of their ability to transcend the particular and embrace the general in human experience. Especially in the case of poetry, to be overly concerned with the historical roots of the literature is to risk missing the point. For whatever else poems exist for, they do not exist primarily to impart information. Appreciation of them is hindered rather than helped by a historical mind-set. Historical matters are therefore not discussed in the context of each chapter.

Secondly, the commentary approaches the poems not only in their own terms, but also in terms of their relation to each other. It is a commentary on the *book* of Lamentations as it now exists. Without making any claims about the circumstances in which the various poems came to be included in the book, then, I shall be paying some attention to the progress of thought which occurs from chapter to chapter, attempting to read each poem in the light of what has gone before. It is the message of the book, and not just of the poems individually, which will be the focus of our interest.

G. OUTLINE OF CONTENTS

COMMENTARY
ON
LAMENTATIONS

NO COMFORT **1:1-22**

The first of the five poems in the book of Lamentations is a vivid and atmospheric depiction of the isolation and grief of a person in mourning. Jerusalem grieves because of the calamity which has befallen her (her defeat by an enemy and the capture of her people), and she does so alone, since her friends (including God) have abandoned her and become her enemies. The terrible nature of her situation is communicated to the reader mainly through pictures drawn from female experience in the ancient world (see further B. B. Kaiser, 'Poet', 174–76). She is vulnerable in the way that widows and conquered princesses are (v. 1); she is despised in the way that women perceived to be unclean are (vv. 8–9, 13, 17); she suffers in the way that a mother does whose children suffer (vv. 5, 16, 18, 20). Repeated reference to the same themes, in particular that of 'no comfort' (vv. 2, 9, 16, 17, 21)—a keynote of this poem which marks it out from the others—emphasises her plight. The overall structure of the poem also contributes to the general effect. The first half, with the exception of the final lines of vv. 9 and 11, is entirely in the third person: a narrator tells us the city's story. The impression created by Zion's sudden interjection in v. 9 is therefore that of a person hitherto kept on the sidelines by this narrator (and thus isolated from the audience as well as from everyone else), who is desperate to make contact and to describe her anguish for herself. Her second interruption in v. 11 is successful, leading on to the speech in vv. 12–16 (vv. 12–15 in 4QLam^a, which has vv. 16–17 in a different order from MT, conforming to the order of the alphabet in chapters 2–4). After a transitional summary by the narrator in v. 17, her second speech follows in vv. 18–22. In the end, then, her isolation is mitigated, though her grief apparently is not. Her aspirations, indeed, seem to be limited to the hope that her enemies will suffer along with her, rather than that she herself will cease to do so (v. 22). In this respect the poem is different from the many other *OT* laments which to a greater or lesser extent end on a note of hope (e.g. Ps. 3, 7, 13, 25, 44, 51, 79, 80). Emphasis is thus given to the darkness of the despair which is felt here.

For a general discussion of the historical circumstances in which this first lament might have been composed, see 'Author, Date and Place of Composition' in the Introduction. It is, happily, unnecessary to know the specific background to the poem in order to appreciate its meaning (see 'Theology' in the Introduction). It is accessible to us simply as the account of the struggles of a suffering individual. The poem invites the reader (along with the other onlookers) to empathise with this individual, to feel the sense of isolation and abandonment which suffering often brings. It further invites us to learn from her experience, to participate in her attempt (and that of those who observe her plight, represented by the narrator) to relate her experience to the reality of God. Suffering, both narrator and sufferer agree, has come about as the result of sin. This is not an explanation of suffering with which a modern reader would always (if at all) be content. The problem of suffering cannot be reduced to simple equations. The last verse of the poem (v. 22) hints, indeed, that the sufferer herself, as opposed to the more detached narrator, has begun to realise this even of her own particular situation. She feels that she is no worse than her enemies, and therefore that the current situation, in which she suffers while they do not, should not be allowed to continue. If we cannot agree that the solution to the problem of suffering which is presented here is particularly satisfactory, however, we are at least reminded in a forceful way of the challenge of suffering to faith, and invited to feel and to ponder its significance. It is a challenge which other *OT* writers take up, including perhaps the author of Isaiah 40–55, who repeatedly assures the people of God that God himself will be their 'comforter' (Isa. 40:1; 49:13; 51:3, 12; 52:9).

*

1. All the ancient translations of Lamentations contain material at the beginning of this verse which claims that the author of the poem, or the book as a whole, was the prophet Jeremiah. LXX, for example, reads: 'And it came to pass, after Israel had gone into captivity and Jerusalem had been laid waste, that Jeremiah sat weeping, and lamented with this lamentation over Jerusalem, and said . . .'. It seems unlikely that any such heading formed part of the original text, since it is not then easy to explain why MT should have omitted all mention of Jeremiah. Whether the tradition about authorship which the various Versional headings reflect is nevertheless correct is, of course, a separate question (see 'Author, Date and Place of Composition' in the Introduction).

How lonely sits the city: Heb. *bādād* (**lonely**) can also mean 'secure' (e.g. Dt. 33:28, Jer. 49:31), and A. Ahuviah, '*'ēkāh yašᵉbāh bādād hāʿîr rabbātî ʿām* (Lam 1:1)', *Beth Mikra* 24 (1979) 423–25, has recently argued that this is its meaning here. The city which once dwelt securely has now become **like a widow**. This is possible, but the loneliness of the city is such a central idea in the poem as a whole that the *RSV* understanding of the word in this context is probably best retained.

full of people: *RSV* adopts the traditional translation, taking the Hebrew *rabbātî* both in this phrase and later in the verse (**great among the nations**) as an adjective meaning, 'much, many, great': thus 'great of people'. McDaniel, 'Studies', 29–31, suggests that it should rather be understood as a noun meaning 'lady, mistress' (cf. the frequent occurrence of *rbt* with this meaning in Phoenician, Ugaritic and Punic). While this would result in slightly better parallelism, if *RSV* punctuation is followed, between the second and third lines of the verse ('mistress' corresponding to **princess**), 'mistress of people' does not make such good sense in the first line as **full of people**, to which use of the adjective we have a parallel in I Sam. 2:5 (Heb. *rabbat bānîm*, 'full of children'). On balance, then, it seems best to understand *rabbātî* in the first line as an adjective, and this being the case, also to regard it as such in the second line. Here *RSV* implies that a new contrast is introduced. The city was once immune, by virtue of her status (**great among the nations**), from the dangers which constantly threaten the weak and unprivileged, but she is no longer so. She is now **like a widow**, and has become as vulnerable as such a person was in the ancient Near East. This interpretation of the Heb., however, gives us a verse which is unbalanced, since the second and third lines then present us with basically the same idea: that one who was great has now lost her status. Moreover, it does not pay sufficient attention to the clue provided by the repetition of *rabbātî* half way through the verse. A better rendering is to be found in *JB*, which understands the verse as comprising two interpretive units rather than three, dividing the second line between them. On this understanding, the verse hinges upon the double use of *rabbātî*: the city was once 'great' in two respects. She was, first of all, 'great' (i.e. **full**) of people: she has now become **like a widow** because she has been bereaved of these. She was, secondly, **great among the nations** and **princess among the cities** (or better, with *JB*, *NEB* and *NIV*, 'provinces', the city being identified with the area around it: the word *mᵉdînāh* is always used elsewhere in the *OT* of the district of a kingdom or empire, as in I Kg. 20:14–15, and especially Ezek. 19:8, where it also appears alongside *gôyīm*, 'nations'). Now, however, she has become **a vassal**. Heb. *mas* usually indicates a relationship between master and servant in which forced labour is imposed on the latter (e.g. I Kg. 5:13 [MT 5:27]), and **vassal** therefore seems rather a weak translation. *NEB*'s 'put to forced labour' or *NIV*'s 'has now become a slave' communicate the meaning more forcibly. The reversal which Jerusalem has suffered is truly a profound one. The princess has become a slave.

2. all her lovers . . . all her friends: although it has been assumed by commentators both ancient (e.g. Targ., where the 'lovers' are idols) and modern (e.g. Hillers, 19, where both 'friends' and 'lovers' are Israel's political allies) that these are friends whom the city sinned in having, nothing in the verse itself justifies such an interpretation. *RSV*'s **lovers** might mislead the modern English-speaking reader in this respect. *NEB*'s 'all that love her' better communicates the sense. Jerusalem's sin is first introduced in v. 5. Here in v. 2 the emphasis is upon the trauma which the loss of 'greatness' (v. 1) has induced—**she weeps bitterly in** (perhaps with the sense 'throughout', cf. Dahood, 'Readings', 174–75) **the night-**; and the isolation in which it must be endured. Not only has the city been deprived of the company of her people, she has also been abandoned by her erstwhile friends. This is a common theme in laments (e.g. Ps. 38:11 [MT 38:12]), and one which recurs throughout this poem in exactly the words found here (*'ēn m^enaḥēm*, **none to comfort**, vv. 9, 17, 21, cf. also v. 16). We may only speculate as to whether the author had a concrete situation in mind, or was simply influenced here by the lament form. Brunet, *Lamentations*, especially on pp. 1–27, attempts to draw a distinction throughout Lamentations 1–4 between the 'foes' (*ṣārîm*) and the **enemies** (*'ōy^ebîm*) of Jerusalem, whom he sees as external (foreign) and internal (Judaean) opponents of the authors respectively. The latter are the erstwhile **friends** of this verse: **they have become her enemies**. Even if this were the correct interpretation of the **friends** and **enemies** here, however, it would not follow that all the **enemies** mentioned in the book must originally have been these **friends**; and careful consideration, indeed, of other such references (1:5, 9, 16, 21; 2:3, 7, 16, 17, 22; 3:46, 52; 4:12) makes clear that it is of foreign enemies of Judah that most of this material is more naturally taken as speaking. The imagery of the first poem, which portrays the city and the inhabitants of Judah and Jerusalem as closely identified (cf. vv. 3, 15, 17), and the latter as being possessed by and dependent upon the former (vv. 4–7, 11, 15–16, 18–19), in any case makes it unlikely that **friends** (which implies a relationship between equals) in this verse does refer to Judaeans. If a concrete situation is in mind, then, it is much more likely that the **friends** who have become **enemies** are cities or states once on good terms with Judah, but now hostile or apathetic towards her (so most commentators).

3. Judah has gone into exile because of affliction and hard servitude: *RSV* takes the Heb. preposition *min* here as causal. Such a translation implies that Judah went **into exile** either to escape harsh conditions at home (i.e. voluntarily: so recently R. B. Salters, 'Lamentations 1:3: Light from the History of Exegesis', in J. D. Martin and P. R. Davies (eds), *A Word in Season: Essays in Honour of William McKane* (JSOTS 42; Sheffield, 1986), 73–89), or as a punishment for inflicting harsh conditions on others (Targ.). *NEB* ('Judah went into the misery of exile and endless servitude') also seems to interpret it as causal, but as indicating the purpose of the exile: 'because of' in the sense of 'so that she may endure'. Gordis, 154, translates the second part of the line '. . . in a state of poverty and oppression', understanding the preposition as a '*mēm* of condition'. *min* is more normally used after the verb *gālāh* 'go into exile', however, in a local sense, 'out of' (cf. I Sam. 4:21–22; Ezek. 12:3; Mic. 1:16). It seems more probable, therefore, that the idea here is that Judah went **into exile** *after having endured* a period **of affliction and hard servitude** (so *JB, NIV*). There seems little need to take the nouns here in a sense different from their normal sense in biblical Heb. (cf. Dahood, 'Readings', 175, who derives *'ny* from *'wn*, 'iniquity': 'Judah went into exile for her iniquity and for the diversity of her worship'; and G. Deiana, 'Interpretazione di Lam. 1, 3a. 7a', *BeO* 23 (1981) 101–3, who derives *'ny* from *'nh*, 'to answer' and *rb* from *ryb* 'to strive, contend': 'Judah went into exile for her arrogance, and for her rebellion went into slavery').

The reference to **Judah**, as Rudolph, 210, rightly points out, is hyperbolic: it means simply that a significant number of Judaeans went into exile. That the author did not think that the entire population had been taken is clear enough from vv. 4, 11, 19–20: some of the priests and the people, at least, remain. Hyperbole is, indeed, a feature of the poem as a whole, a fact which must be borne in mind when the attempt is made to look behind the text to the historical circumstances which might have prompted its composition (see 'Author, Date and Place of Composition' in the Introduction). The language is impressionistic rather than scientifically precise.

she dwells now among the nations: there is no Heb. word to which the English 'now' corresponds. *RSV* is interpreting the phrase as referring to the present plight of Judah in exile, where she has yet found no respite from her troubles. Some commentators (so Rudolph, 211–12; Hillers, 6–7) have rather argued that it refers to the past, when Judah still 'dwelt among the nations' as an independent entity. The idea would then be, as Hillers puts it, '. . . that the actual catastrophe came after a long period of inglorious trouble and toil', in which Judah was harassed by the surrounding nations. This interpretation is not entirely satisfactory, however, since the contrast which has been noted in vv. 1-2 between the past (when Judah/Jerusalem was 'princess among the provinces') and the present is thereby destroyed. The first line of the verse by itself does not imply a long period of affliction, and may be taken as referring only to the immediate circumstances of the catastrophe. It seems best, then, to retain the *RSV* interpretation. It may be noted, indeed, that in this case the contrast between past and present is actually enhanced: Jerusalem 'sits (Heb. *yāš^ebāh*) alone', bereaved of her people, because her people (i.e. Judah) **dwells** (Heb. *yāš^ebāh*) **now among the nations.**

in the midst of her distress: the word *mēṣar* which is here rendered **distress** derives from a verb which can mean 'to be cramped, narrow', and *JB*'s 'in places where there is no way out' may be a more satisfactory rendering here. Although Judah has now moved her dwelling-place, she has been relentlessly pursued by those who have afflicted her and is now hemmed in.

4. After the brief description of the fate of the people in v. 3, we return here to the situation in which Jerusalem finds herself as a result. The consequences for religious worship are specifically in view: **none come to the appointed feasts.** The **roads** which in the past would have carried pilgrims to the city are therefore in mourning, while the **gates** which would have been one of the focal points of its life **are desolate.** This latter English expression is, of course, ambiguous, since **desolate** can mean, among other things, both 'uninhabited' (cf. *JB*'s 'deserted') and 'wretched'. The Heb. root (*šmm*) which lies behind this translation is similarly ambiguous. The context in this instance—the **roads** mourning, the **priests** groaning, the city suffering bitterly (an expression which is best taken, in view of the similar constructions in Ru. 1:13 and 2 Kg. 4:27, as referring to suffering internally experienced: cf. *NIV*'s 'she is in bitter anguish')— might lead us to expect the participation of the **gates** in the lamentation, and to regard the verb here as describing their *attitude* rather than the circumstances in which they find themselves. An appropriate translation might then be 'all her gates are in despair' (cf. *JB*'s rendering of the almost identical verbal form in Lam. 1:16—'my sons are in despair').

Much depends, however, upon the reading which is adopted in the first part of the final line. *RSV*'s **her maidens have been dragged away** follows LXX, which seems to presuppose a Heb. verb $n^e\hat{h}\hat{u}g\hat{o}t$, 'led away' (cf. 4QLam^a). Young women are often mentioned in the OT (e.g. Jg. 21:19–21, Jer. 31:13, Ps. 68:25 [MT 68:26]) as having a role in festal celebrations, and their absence might be understood as particularly symbolic of Jerusalem's plight. If this reading is followed, then **desolate** is best understood in the sense of 'deserted', the absence of the maidens being a particular example of this general situation: 'all her gates are deserted, her priests groan; her maidens have been dragged away, and she herself is in bitter anguish'. MT, on the other hand, reads $n\hat{u}g\hat{o}t$, which is usually taken to be a form of the verb $y\bar{a}g\bar{a}h$, 'to suffer' which appears in Lam. 1:5, 1:12, 3:32, 33. Given the context, this is most probably a reference to grief (cf. *NIV, JB*), in which case all the verbs of the second and third lines are best taken as describing the reactions of the various parties to the bereavement already described in vv. 1–4a: 'all her gates are in despair, her priests groan; her maidens grieve, and she herself is in bitter anguish'. There is little to choose between the two possibilities.

Whether the first line of the verse implies the complete cessation of religious festivals, as some commentators (e.g. Peake, 303–4) have argued, must be open to question. The language of the remainder is clearly not precise, whichever understanding of it is adopted. The city cannot be completely 'deserted' if there are **priests** in it waiting for pilgrims and people in it searching for food (v. 11), nor can all the **maidens** be grieving if some of them have 'gone into captivity' (v. 18). **None come to the appointed feasts** may therefore be an exaggeration.

5. her foes have become the head: this may be an allusion to Dt. 28:13, 44, where Israel is told that obedience to God will lead to dominance over others and disobedience to their dominance over her: 'he shall be the head and you shall be the tail' (Dt. 28:44). Certainly the link is clearly made in our present verse between the state in which Jerusalem now finds herself and her wrongdoing: **the LORD has made her suffer for the multitude of her**

transgressions. Again the theme of bereavement recurs: **her children** (i.e. probably Judaeans in general rather than young people in particular) **have gone away, captives before the foe**. Brunet, *Lamentations*, 8, of course, distinguishes between the **foes**, who have the chief position and give orders (**have become the head**), and the Judaean **enemies**, who **prosper** under their patronage (cf. the comment on v. 1). The more natural way in which to interpret this part of the verse is clearly to take both *ṣārîm* and *ʾōyᵉbîm* as undifferentiated terms for the foreign enemies who have taken the people captive.

6. daughter of Zion: in the Heb. *bat ṣîyôn*, as in the many other phrases containing *bat* or *bᵉtûlat bat* ('virgin daughter') in Lamentations, the first word is in apposition to the second. A better translation, then, and one which avoids any possible misunderstanding, would be 'daughter Zion'. See Hillers, xxxvii–xxxix, for a good brief discussion. From Zion has departed **all her majesty**, perhaps a reference to the **princes** of the next line (Dahood, 'Readings', 175–176). Since 'prince' has a precise connotation in modern English (i.e. the son of a king) which is not intended by Heb. *śār*, a better translation would be the more general 'leaders' (*JB*). These leaders are depicted by *RSV*, which along with *NEB* and *NIV* follows MT here, as **harts** or stags fleeing before the hunter. They **find no pasture**, and are consequently weak, fleeing **without strength**: their situation is hopeless, their capture by **the pursuer** (Heb. *rôdēp*) inevitable. There is a parallel here, of course, with v. 3, where Judah is depicted as being harried relentlessly by her 'pursuers' (*rōdᵉpeyhā*). *JB*, on the other hand, takes its cue from LXX in reading 'rams' instead of *harts*, retaining the consonants of MT (*ʾylym*), but vocalizing them as *ʾêlîm* instead of *ʾayyālîm*. The understanding of the metaphor is thus rather different: the leaders have already been captured and are like sheep 'driven by the drover'.

7. This verse is quite a bit longer than the others in chapter 1, as can readily be seen even from *RSV*. Most commentators have for this reason argued that the original material must have been expanded by a later editor. The majority have thought that **all the**

precious things . . . days of old is the most likely addition (so Kraus, 22; Plöger, 134; Kaiser, 318, n. 59; Brandscheidt, *Gotteszorn und Menschenleid*, 74; cf. the omission of this line in *JB* and *NEB*), although a few have favoured **When her people . . . to help her** (so Rudolph, 206, Albrektson, *Studies*, 62–63, Gottlieb, *Study*, 13). There is, however, no textual or literary-critical evidence to indicate that either of these lines as a unit is secondary. The Qumran ms. 4QLam[a] does have a slightly shorter text for the first two lines taken together ('Remember, O LORD, all our sufferings which were from days of old'), but the relationship of this text to MT and the Versions, which presuppose the longer form, is obscure (see Cross, 'Studies', 130, 134 for the text and 140–41 for an attempt at an explanation), and it does not seem that we can deduce anything about the original length of the stanza from it. Nor can we be sure, given the tentative nature of our knowledge concerning the conventions governing ancient Hebrew poetry, that a longer stanza could not have been inserted by the original author of the poem. Indeed, Freedman, 'Acrostics and Metrics', 374, has recently argued on metrical grounds that all the lines of the stanza are necessary. A stanza of similar length, it should be noted, is found in 2:19, where there is just as little justification for any abbreviation.

affliction and bitterness: *RSV*'s **bitterness** assumes that MT is corrupt, the Heb. letter *r* having become confused with the similar-looking *d*, and reads *merôreyhā* instead of MT *merûdeyhā*. There is no Versional support for such a reading, however. Indeed, although there are differing perceptions of their meaning, the consonants of MT probably lie behind all the Versions. Targ., Vulg., and perhaps Syr. (although it is ambiguous: see Albrektson, *Studies*, 60–61) appear to link the word with the verb *mārad*, 'to rebel', an interpretation which seems unlikely in the context. LXX's 'rejection, thrusting away', on the other hand, may be the result of connecting it with the verb *rûd*, 'to wander restlessly, roam'. The Masoretes, too, may have had a connection with *rûd* in mind: *NEB*'s 'misery and wandering', and *NIV*'s 'affliction and wandering' both link MT's *merûdeyhā* with this root. The problem with both the LXX interpretation and that of these translations, however, is that elsewhere in this poem it is always the people, not the city, who are on the move. Zion remains behind to mourn. She is therefore unlikely to be recalling her own wandering. Meek, 9, proposes that a different verbal root (*rdd*, 'to beat down, subdue') lies behind our word, and translates it 'oppression'. One might appeal to Isa. 45:1, Ps. 144:2 and Syr. in support of such a possibility. The view adopted here is that the plural *merûdeyhā* is best taken, like the plural *merûdîm* in Isa. 58:7, as referring to wandering people—people of no fixed abode, homeless people: 'Jerusalem remembers in the days of her affliction and her homeless ones . . .'. A distinction exists in this line, as it does in the remainder of the verse (cf. **When her people fell into the hand of the foe . . . the foe gloated over her**) and the chapter, between the fate of the city and and that of her people.

all the precious things that were hers from days of old: the **precious things** (Heb. *maḥᵃmudeyhā*) may simply be everything in general which the city had in the past (cf. Targ.'s 'all her luxuries') and has now lost, or something in particular such as temple treasure, to which 1:10 may also allude. We might also translate this word 'precious ones', however, again interpreting the line as referring to the people who once inhabited the city (cf. Lam. 2:4, where *maḥᵃmaddê* certainly refers to people rather than to things). Such an interpretation fits the context well.

mocking at her downfall: Heb. *mišbāt*, translated **downfall**, occurs only here in the *OT*. Several of our older witnesses derive it from the verb *yāšab*, 'to sit, dwell', rendering 'settlement, dwelling' (most of the LXX texts, Aq.), while others seem to link it with *šābāh*, 'to take captive' (Codex Alexandrinus' 'deportation, captivity', cf. Targ.). The latter reading does not fit the context well (cf. the comments on the first part of this verse), while the idea of the foe mocking Jerusalem's 'dwelling-place' seems very strange. It seems more likely that the word is derived from *šābat*, 'to cease, desist' (cf. the improbable 'sabbaths' of Vulg. and *AV*), and is to be understood as referring to the city's reduced state: thus *RSV*'s rendering and *NEB*'s 'fallen state'. It is not clear in the nature of the case whether the city's 'destruction' (*NIV*) is implied by the word, nor by 4QLam^a's *mišbāreyhā*.

8-9. therefore she became filthy: Heb. *nîdāh*, translated **filthy**, is found only here in the *OT*. It is taken by Aq., Syr. and most modern interpreters to be a variant form of *niddāh*, 'impurity', a noun which appears in Lam. 1:17 and which is used elsewhere especially of female impurity (Lev. 15:19–33). Some commentators, however, have connected the word with the root *nwd*, and indeed the reading *nwd* is actually found in 4QLam^a (see Cross, 'Studies', 130, 134, 141). In the Qal this can mean 'to move to and fro' (cf. LXX's 'a tossing motion') or 'to wander' (cf. Targ., which interprets the word as referring to the exile), and in the Hiphil of Jer. 18:16 it means 'to shake' the head, apparently in horror or derision (cf. Ps. 44:14 [MT 44:15]). The latter usage has led, on the one hand, to the suggestion that we should understand *nîdāh* (or *nwd* in 4QLam^a) as meaning 'one at whom the head is shaken, object of scorn'. It is not easy to see how either of these words could mean '*object* of scorn', however, even if it were granted that the word of itself could express the idea of 'shaking the *head*'. In Jer. 18:16 and Ps. 44:14 the actual word 'head' (*rō'š*) is required in order to define what it is that is being shaken. The notion of Jerusalem as a wanderer or exile, on the other hand, does not fit the context well (see the comment on v. 7). The idea of the city's impurity does accord well, however, both with the immediate and wider context. Acceptance of the reading *nîdāh* and its interpretation as a variant of *niddāh* therefore seems best. In the immediate context we find two other terms, *'erwāh*, **nakedness** and *ṭum'āh*, **uncleanness**, which are used elsewhere in the *OT*, often closely associated with *niddāh*, in statements about ritual cleanness and uncleanness. Of particular interest is Lev. 18:19, where all three appear: 'You shall not approach a woman to uncover her nakedness while she is in her menstrual uncleanness (lit. 'in the impurity of her uncleanness)'. For any individual to have their **nakedness** uncovered by the wrong person was very shameful in Heb. thought, and a plethora of rules (e.g. Lev. 18:6–18) dealt with such matters. Imagery deriving from these rules is used elsewhere in the *OT* to describe the shame of the conquered (e.g. Isa. 47:3; Jer. 13:26; and Nah. 3:5, where **skirts** are lifted to expose nakedness). Here in Lam. 1:8–9, the precise picture is that of Jerusalem openly viewed by her erstwhile friends (**All who honoured her**) while she is in a state of *niddāh*, 'impurity', as a result of her sins. They have **seen** both **her nakedness** and, perhaps, her bloodstained clothing (**her uncleanness was in her skirts**). The consequence is that they now **despise her**, and have abandoned her in the face of the enemy (**she has no comforter**). It is her impure state, then, which explains the attitude and behaviour of her old acquaintances referred to at other points in the poem (e.g. v. 2).

yea, she herself groans and turns her face away: McDaniel, 'Studies', 31-32, and Hillers, 10, object that the normal understanding of Hebrew *gam* ('also, too', here translated **yea**) is inappropriate in this context. It is difficult to see the force of this argument. The thought is that it is not only others who despise Jerusalem: even she cannot bear to look at herself. There is no need, then, to have recourse to a possible Heb. *gam*, 'loud', corresponding to the Ugaritic *gm*. There must be some doubt, indeed, as to the existence of such a form anywhere in the *OT* (see Gottlieb, *Study*, 14, n. 33).

she took no thought of her doom: Heb. *ʾaḥᵃrîtāh*, **her doom**, is better translated more neutrally as 'her future' (*NIV*), i.e. 'she did not consider the consequences for herself' of falling into impurity. Gordis, 156, prefers the translation 'she does not remember her children', noting the likely meaning of *ʾaḥᵃrît* in Ezek. 23:25, Am. 4:2 *et al*. This is not, however, likely to be the intended meaning in view of 1:7 ('Jerusalem remembers . . .').

therefore her fall is terrible: lit. 'and she came down wondrously' (*wattēred pᵉlāʾîm*). *RSV*'s **therefore** is best avoided (cf. *JB, NEB, NIV*), since the text is not likely to mean that the city's lack of foresight has affected the nature of her 'coming down'. Heb. *yārad*, 'to come down', is found in Dt. 20:20 of the *fall* of a city and in Isa. 47:1 and Ezek. 30:6 of the *humiliation* of Babylon and Egypt respectively. Both ideas, fall and humiliation, would fit the context here. It should be noted, however, that LXX ('she has

lowered her haughty tones') appears to have read the verb as a
Hiphil (*wattōred*) rather than a Qal (*wattēred*). If a Hiphil was indeed
intended by the author, and given that *wattōred* can be understood
as a second person masculine as well as a third person feminine
singular verb, a better rendering might be 'you (i.e. Yahweh) have
brought down judgements'. The sudden change to the direct form
of address to God which this interpretation would require is not
unparalleled in this poem (cf. v. 10) and it does have the advantage
of allowing us to take Heb. *pele*', 'wonder, extraordinary thing'
(often found in the *OT* of God's acts of judgement and redemption,
e.g. Exod. 15:11) in its natural sense. The Massoretic pointing,
in contrast, requires us to take *pᵉlāʾim* in an adverbial sense, a
sense in which this noun is not found elsewhere in the OT. Even
if this pointing is followed, however, the implication of the use of
pᵉlāʾim is still that Jerusalem's fall is not only extraordinary (in
that it was unexpected, perhaps, or in its extent), but also an act
of God's judgement.

O LORD, behold my affliction: OL (followed by *NEB*) has
'her affliction', making the speaker the same as in the remainder
of the verse. It seems probable, however, that this unsupported
reading is an attempt to smooth out a perceived difficulty, and that
we should retain **my affliction** with the majority of texts. Jerusalem
herself speaks for the first time, interjecting this cry of anguish into
the description by the observer. She will have more opportunity
to speak for herself later in the poem.

10. over all her precious things: the allusion may be to **precious
things** in general, of which the main one is **her sanctuary**; or to
precious things contained in the latter (i.e. temple treasure). It
may also be to the people of the city ('her precious ones': see the
comment on 1:7): **the enemy** has not only entered the city to seize
people, he has also violated **her sanctuary**.

those whom thou didst forbid to enter thy congregation: the
allusion here is apparently to Dt. 23:3 [MT 23:4], though it need
not be imagined that our author is thinking here only of Ammonites
and Moabites. More probably the prohibition is being interpreted
broadly as referring to foreigners in general (cf. Ezek. 44:9, Neh.

13:1-3). It is interesting to note that the observer here addresses God directly for the first and only time (but see the comment on v. 9) in this poem. **to enter thy congregation** is, literally, 'they shall not enter the congregation to you'. 4QLam[a] lacks 'the congregation to you' and the first part of the next verse up to 'precious things', apparently through accidental omission. *RSV* interprets the whole phrase as indirect speech and takes 'to you' (*lāk*) in the sense of 'belonging to you', therefore **thy** (the interpretation also of LXX, Syr. and Targ.). This is perfectly possible grammatically (*contra* Albrektson, *Studies*, 65–66; cf. GKC §129b). It would also be possible, however, to understand it as the words of Yahweh in direct speech, taking *lāk* as referring to Israel (so Albrektson), or even to retain it as indirect speech and translate: 'to enter before you in the congregation'.

11. All her people groan as they search for bread: the aftermath of the fall of the city is famine, and the people, like the priests (v. 4) and the city herself (vv. 8, 21), **groan** in misery. The situation is such that they **they trade their treasures for food**. 4QLam[a] and LXX actually have 'her treasures', implying that the people sold off the treasures mentioned in the previous verse (and thus that these treasures are being interpreted as the temple treasures), but **their treasures** seems to fit the context better. It is not clear, however, whether we are to understand these to be possessions or offspring. The Hebrew word is the same as that in v. 10, and could be rendered 'precious ones'. The same word is found in Hos. 9:16, where *RSV* translates '. . . I will slay their beloved children'. The practice of selling children in order to survive was not unknown in the ancient world (see Hillers, 25–26, for examples and references), as it is not unknown in modern times. **to revive their strength** is a possible translation of the rather vague Heb. *lᵉhāšîb nāpeš*, 'to bring back the soul', but in this context, as in v. 19, *NIV*'s 'to keep themselves alive' is perhaps better.

Look, O LORD, and behold, for I am despised: some of the Greek mss. read '. . . for she is despised', but the change of person fits the change of subject matter (from people to city) better, and provides the transition to the first person speech which now follows.

Zion reminds God that she is **despised** by those who once honoured her (cf. v. 8).

12. Is it nothing to you . . .?: MT has simply *lô> ʿᵃlêkem* 'not to you', and the *RSV* rendering of this phrase is somewhat strained. Many scholars, indeed, have maintained that the phrase is untranslatable, and have suspected a corrupt text. All the ancient Versions may be taken as reflecting the consonants of MT, however, although LXX and Vulg. seem to have read the first word as *lû>*, 'if, O that!' instead of *lô>*. This alternative does not seem to help us to make much sense of the phrase in the context. Nor does the *>ēlay* (for MT's *ʿᵃlêkem*) of 4QLamᵃ. Among the better attempts at translation of MT as it stands are those of Albrektson, *Studies*, 66–69, and Gottlieb, *Study*, 15–17, both of whom take *lô> ʿᵃlêkem* as a statement rather than a question: '(it is) not for you', i.e. 'this is nothing which concerns you'. Albrektson goes on to suggest that **all you who pass by** refers to the 'ordinary man' ('this does not happen to everybody', the disaster is unparalleled), while Gottlieb more plausibly argues that these are the onlookers who are often found in lament psalms and from whom mockery may be expected (e.g. Ps. 89:41 [MT 89:42]). His understanding of *lô> ʿᵃlêkem* as a rejection of such mockery, however ('it does not concern any of you who pass by'), does not fit well with the invitation to the onlookers to **look and see**. Both these attempts are therefore in the end unsatisfactory. The ancient Jewish rendering of the phrase as 'may it not come upon you' (cf. Gordis, 157) also does not fit the context very well. What we require here is a satisfactory link between the two invitations to **look** which occur in vv. 11 and 12. A better approach, therefore, is to retain the interrogative but to understand 'is it not for you?' in the sense of 'does this situation not exist for your sake?' The thought is that God has inflicted the disaster precisely so that the the onlookers may view its consequences (cf. the comments on v. 18). The invitation to **look** at Jerusalem's state then follows quite naturally.

13. In this and the following verses, the onlookers are given further information about the city's suffering, so that they may make their assessment. **From on high he sent fire; into my bones he**

made it descend: MT reads 'from on high he sent fire into my bones and he/it had dominion over her/it' (*wayyirdennāh*). *RSV*'s translation, which is based on the LXX reading, ignores the 'and' and reads the second verb as *yôrīdennāh* or *yôrīdennû* (**he made it descend:** cf. also 4QLamᵃ) rather than *yirdennāh*. There is also ancient Versional support (Symm., Syr., Vulg.) for a first rather than a third person suffix on this verb ('He brought me down'). MT has been interpreted (so Driver, 'Hebrew Notes', 137) as meaning 'and it (the **fire**) overcame them (the **bones**)'. In this case the normally feminine noun *'ēš* governs a masculine verb, as in Jer. 48:45 and Ps. 104:4, and the verbal suffix *ennāh*, although singular, refers back to a plural noun, *'aṣmōtay*. A much more natural way in which to understand the Heb., however, is to take Yahweh as the subject of both verbs: he controlled the fire after sending it. The idea in all cases is that Yahweh is directly responsible for the suffering of the victim (cf. Jer. 20:9 for a slightly different use of the picture of 'fire in the bones'). **Fire** from heaven is, of course, frequently associated with God's judgement elsewhere in the *OT* (e.g. 2 Kg. 1:10, 12, 14). The imagery here therefore neatly combines the thoughts that Jerusalem is suffering, and that this suffering is the outworking of Yahweh's judgement.

he spread a net for my feet; he turned me back: another metaphor is now used, that of the hunter spreading his **net** in order to ensnare his prey. **he turned me back** (Heb. *hešîbanî 'āḥôr*) probably refers in this context to the prey's action in avoiding the trap: the picture is of a victim harried by the hunter (cf. vv. 3, 6). There may also be allusions in the use of this phrase, however, both to defeat by enemy armies (cf. *tešîbēnû 'āḥôr* in Ps. 44:10 [MT 44:11]) and to the shameful state of Jerusalem in v. 8 (where *wattāšob 'āḥôr*, 'and she turned back', is plausibly rendered by *RSV* 'and turns her face away'). Elsewhere in the OT the image of 'spreading the net' is often used of the enemy's assault on the righteous (e.g. Ps. 35:7) or of Yahweh's action against his enemies (Hos. 7:12). That Jerusalem should be the object of Yahweh's attention in this respect is a shocking reversal of the norms, emphasizing the dire plight in which the city finds itself.

he has left me stunned, faint all the day long: there is a further allusion to vv. 8 and 9 in the Heb. *dāwāh*, translated here (rather euphemistically) as faint. In Lev. 15:33 and 20:18 this adjective describes the state of menstrual impurity. This being the case, Heb. *šōmēmāh* (**stunned**) is better translated 'desolate' (cf. *RSV*'s rendering of *šōmēmîn* in v. 4, and the comments on 'desolate' there), and the whole line taken as referring back to, and holding Yahweh responsible for, the city's impure state. *NEB*'s 'he made me an example of desolation, racked with sickness all day long' is a better attempt, so long as it is remembered which 'sickness' is being talked about.

14. My transgressions were bound into a yoke; by his hand they were fastened together: the question of original text is particularly difficult here. MT has *nišqad ʿōl pᵉšāʿay*, which is unclear because the root *šqd* appears nowhere else in the *OT*. Some Heb. mss. read *šqd* instead, and this is reflected in some of the Versions. LXX seems to presuppose a text *nišqad ʿal pᵉšāʿay*, 'watch was kept over my sins'; Syr. a text *nišqᵉdû ʿalay pᵉšāʿay*, 'my sins were stirred up against me'; and Vulg. a text *nišqad ʿōl pᵉšāʿay*, understanding this as 'he watched over the yoke of my sins'. Targ., on the other hand, has 'the yoke of my rebellion is heavy', implying the Heb. root *qšh* (cf. *JB*'s 'the yoke of my sins weighs down on me'); while 4QLamᵃ, which is apparently to be translated as 'the yoke of my transgressions was bound on', reflects *qšr* (so also *NEB*). Interestingly enough, Ewald, 108, long ago suggested that MT's *šqd* itself might well be a technical term for the binding on of a yoke. The problem with all these readings, however, is that they do not make very good sense when taken with what follows in the remainder of the stanza. **by his hand they were fastened** (or better 'woven', with *NIV*) **together** is clearly best taken as concerning the *construction* of a yoke out of the raw materials (the **transgressions**). This yoke is then put in place upon the **neck**, and its burden, or perhaps the hard work which ensues, produces fatigue: **he** (or perhaps 'it') **caused my strength to fail**. The parallelism which is so often found in Hebrew poetry leads us to expect that the first part of the first line ought, like the second part, to tell us of the yoke's construction. Perhaps, then, the best we can do is simply to guess the meaning of MT's *śqd* from the context, as *RSV* and *NIV* have done. Clearly *pᵉśā'ay* cannot, however, be the subject of the clause, as these versions have it. If we are to retain MT, I would suggest the following: 'a yoke was fashioned out of my transgressions'. This is, however, only a guess.

the Lord gave me into the hands of those whom I cannot withstand: the idea might be that God has given Jerusalem over to her enemies in the weakened state which the burden of the yoke has produced. Alternatively, we might understand Heb. *qûm* (**withstand**) in its more literal sense of 'arise', and imagine that it is the power of the transgressions which is in view. The city's strength has failed under their weight, and she is no longer able to 'arise' from the ground.

15. The Lord flouted all my mighty men: the Heb. root *slh* (**flouted**) is quite rare, occurring apart from this verse only in Ps. 119:118 and Job 28:16. In the latter reference, it is used of measuring the worth of something (wisdom) in gold. In the former, it seems to have the sense of 'to evaluate negatively', i.e. 'to have contempt for, to scorn'. The translations of *RSV* and *NEB* ('treated with scorn') are therefore to be preferred over those of LXX ('cut off, remove'), Syr. ('tread down, subdue', cf. *AV*), *JB* ('spurned') and *NIV* ('rejected'). Like an enemy commander, God has weighed up the opposition and found them of no account. He has therefore **summoned an assembly** against them, in order to destroy them. There is neither support from the Versions nor any need for *NEB*'s repointing of MT *mô'ēd* (**assembly**) as *mô'ād*, 'rank on rank'. The use of *mô'ēd* is explained by the context. It regularly denotes a religious festival, such as Sukkoth (Dt. 31:10)—usually a time of rejoicing for the participants. This is its meaning, for example, in 1:4: God's actions against Zion have affected the celebration of 'the appointed feasts'. In their stead, v. 15 tells us, he has arranged another **assembly**, one with hostile intent. As grapes would be crushed in the **wine press** after their harvesting, so on this occasion Zion's **young men**, and indeed the whole population of Judah (**the virgin daughter (of) Judah**, cf. the comment on v. 6) have been crushed.

16. The first of Jerusalem's speeches ends with a description of how the events recounted in vv. 11c–15 make her and her people feel. Because of these things, she claims, **my eyes flow with tears**. MT reads 'my eye, my eye flows with water'. Heb. idiom regularly refers to one of a pair where we might refer to both (cf. Ps. 88:9 [MT 88:10], 'my eye grows dim through sorrow'). Repetition for reasons of emphasis or style is also not unknown (see Gottlieb, *Study*, 19), and we should therefore hesitate before taking the easy course here (with many commentators) of regarding the second 'my eye' as the result of scribal error ('dittography', accidental duplication of the same word), or the first as the result of textual corruption (e.g. McDaniel, 'Studies', 32–33) or Massoretic misunderstanding of the consonantal text (Dahood, 'Readings', 178–179). 'My eyes, my eyes flow with tears' has a certain pathos which *RSV* and some of the ancient Versions lack. The pain of her isolation is once more stressed with reference to the lack of a **comforter** (cf. vv. 2 and 9). If there were one, he might **revive her courage**, or perhaps even 'keep her alive'. The Heb. expression here is the same as that in vv. 11 and 19 (translated by *RSV* 'to revive the strength'), and the thought may be that the pain of her isolation has caused her to lose the will to live. Her **children** (i.e. the people) are in a similar frame of mind: **desolate** (cf. comment on v. 4) because of the enemy victory.

17. The narrator breaks in again for a moment, his contribution acting as a transitional piece between Jerusalem's first and second speeches. He picks up the theme of isolation. **Zion stretches out her hands**, perhaps in prayer (*NEB*) but more probably (in view of vv. 2, 8–9) in supplication to those who view her plight. She seeks a response from them, but none is forthcoming: there is none to comfort her. In vv. 2, 8–9, as we have seen, a reversal is described. Jerusalem's friends have become her enemies, and those who once honoured her now despise her. The same reversal is probably described in the second line of this verse (**that his neighbours should be his foes**, cf. also *NIV*), though we might also translate Heb. *sᵉbîbâw ṣārâw* as 'foes from every side' (*JB*, cf. also LXX, Syr., *AV, NEB*). Another theme picked up from vv.

8–9 is that of the city's 'uncleanness' (Heb. *niddāh*, *RSV*'s **filthy thing**), the reason for her rejection by her erstwhile friends (cf. the comments on vv. 8–9). An additional cause for this is introduced here by most texts, however: **the LORD has commanded** it. 4QLam[a] differs in reading the verb as *sph*, 'to keep watch', which Cross, 'Studies', 147, prefers, but which does not seem to make such good sense in the context.

18–19. The LORD is in the right, for I have rebelled against his word: the first line of v. 18 could be interpreted as stating either that Yahweh is justified in his actions because the city has sinned (*RSV, JB, NEB*); or that the city has sinned in spite of the fact that Yahweh is righteous (cf. *NIV*'s 'yet I rebelled . . .'). Whichever translation is adopted, the second line is best taken as an invitation to the **peoples** to learn from her mistake. They are invited to **hear** and, as in v. 12, to **behold** the city's **suffering** (Heb. *reʾû makʾōbî*, cf. *reʾû ʾim-yēš makʾōb kemakʾōbî* in v. 12, rendered by *RSV* as 'see if there is any sorrow like my sorrow'). *RSV*'s **but** at the beginning of the line, which is not implied by the Heb., is therefore not a very helpful insertion, and is best omitted.

my maidens and my young men . . .: in the remainder of vv. 18–19 those addressed are once more reminded, by the reintroduction of earlier themes, of the situation in which Jerusalem finds herself. The **maidens** have already been mentioned in v. 4, where they were either 'dragged away 'or mourning (see the comment on v. 4), the **young men** in v. 15, where they were 'crushed'. The treachery of the **lovers** was commented upon in v. 2, and the famine described in v. 11, although here the focus is upon the **priests and elders** rather than the people as a whole, and here for the first time we are told of deaths as a result of it: **they perished in the city.** *NEB*'s weaker 'they went hungry' gives the root *gwʿ* a sense which is found in Arabic but not in Biblical Heb., and it is unlikely to be correct. Nor is there any justification for *NEB*'s placing of the addition 'and could find nothing' (which is based on LXX, cf. also Syr.) immediately after this verb: if this phrase is to be read, it must rather be read at the end of the verse where LXX and Syr. have it, and where it makes little difference to its meaning.

20. As in vv. 11-12 the invitation to 'look' was first extended to God (v. 11c, Heb. *rᵉʾēh*) and then to the onlookers (v. 12, Heb. *rᵉʾû*), so here the invitation to the peoples to 'behold' (Heb. *rᵉʾû*) in v. 18 is followed now by one to God: **Behold** (Heb. *rᵉʾēh*), **O LORD, for I am in distress**, or perhaps 'See, LORD, how distressed I am', cf. *JB, NEB, NIV*). A description of the distress follows: **my soul is in tumult**. Heb. *mēʿîm* (often lit. 'stomach, womb', here rendered **soul**) is conceived elsewhere in the *OT* as the seat of the emotions, and is probably to be given this metaphorical connotation here, although *JB* ('my entrails shudder') and *NEB* ('my bowels writhe in anguish') prefer a more literal rendering. The thought is that the emotions are in an extremely unsettled state. The Heb. root *ḥmr* which lies behind *RSV*'s **in tumult** is used elsewhere in the *OT* of liquid in an agitated condition (a heavy sea in Ps. 46:3 [MT 46:4]; fermenting wine in Ps. 75:8 [MT 75:9]). We might well render the phrase as 'my emotions are in turmoil'.

my heart is wrung within me: lit. 'my heart is turned within me'. *RSV* (as well as *NEB, NIV*) suggests that this refers, like the phrase in the first line, simply to a *state*, viz. turmoil in the emotions. Analogous expressions in Exod. 14:5 and Hos. 11:8, however, suggest rather that we should understand the emphasis here as upon a *change of state*, from one attitude or state of mind to another. We might then translate 'my heart has changed', either linking this with **because I have been very rebellious** (i.e. it is Zion's rebellion which has resulted in the loss of equanimity described in v. 20a), or breaking the line in two and taking the rebellion as the cause of the events described in the third line (so, for example, Rudolph, 208). The objection of C.L. Seow, 'A Textual Note on Lamentations 1:20', *CBQ* 47 (1985) 416–19, to the former interpretation—that elsewhere in the *OT* emotional stress for the rebels is never said to be the *direct* result of their rebellion— seems somewhat pedantic, since a connection of this *general* type between sin and suffering *is* often made elsewhere. The evidence of the Versions (LXX, Syr. and Vulg.) does suggest, nevertheless, that he may be correct in his claim that the Heb. root *mrr*, 'be bitter', rather than *mrh*, 'be rebellious', originally appeared here: 'how bitter I am!'.

In the street the sword bereaves; in the house it is like death: the third line returns to the immediate human cause of the distress. The *RSV* translation may imply either that the situation **in the house** is **like death**, or that **the sword** resembles death in that it causes bereavement. The former interpretation is perhaps more likely to be correct than the latter, particularly in view of texts like Jer. 14:18 and Ezek. 7:15. Two different aspects of the city's plight are in mind: the death of some of the inhabitants and the severe suffering (it is **like death**) of those who remain alive. There is no need to introduce the notion of an emphatic k^e or $k\hat{i}$ here (cf. Gordis, 159; Dahood, 'Readings', 179), nor to accept a meaning for Heb. *kmwt* which cannot be established from the rest of the *OT* (cf. *NEB*'s 'plague'; and F. Perles, 'Was bedeutet *kmwt* Threni 1, 20?', *OLZ* 23 (1920) 157–58, who links *kmwt* with an Akkadian word meaning 'captivity').

21. Hear how I groan: *RSV* here follows LXX and Syr. in taking the verb as an imperative. It should be noted, however, that LXX has a *plural* imperative, and thus appears to regard the subject of the address as the 'peoples' of v. 18. This is unlikely to be correct, and since LXX clearly reads the consonants of MT, which is further supported by Vulg. and Targ., MT's 'they have heard how I groan' is best retained (with *NIV*, but against *JB, NEB* and most commentators). It makes perfectly good sense, in the context of the address to God, either as an indefinite reference to others (cf. *NIV*'s 'People have heard my groaning') or as a reference to the **enemies** referred to in the next line.

All my enemies have heard of my trouble: the **enemies** of Jerusalem are more broadly defined on this occasion than they were in vv. 5, 9 and 16, where they were active in causing her trouble. Here the author is concerned even with those who were not directly involved and have only **heard** about it.

bring thou the day thou hast announced: *RSV* again follows Syr. (as do *JB* and *NEB*) rather than MT, which all the other Versions support in reading the verb as a perfect rather than an imperative. *NIV*, on the other hand, regards MT's perfect as itself referring to the future, understanding it as a precative perfect, 'May you bring' (cf. Gordis, 160). A past tense ('you have brought') is, however, certainly more likely in the context, since the 'day' with which the first poem (cf. v. 12), and indeed also the second (cf. 2:1, 7, 16, 21–22), is otherwise concerned is clearly the day of judgement on Israel rather than the day of judgement upon her enemies. The first part of the line is best taken, then, as a reference to the present situation. The enemies are glad because 'the day' has come (cf. in particular 2:16). The latter part of the line (**let them be as I am**) is more difficult. Albrektson, *Studies*, 83–84, understands it as introducing the idea (the future judgement of the enemies) which is elaborated upon in v. 22 : 'you have brought the day which you announced—but they shall be as I am'. It is more natural, however, to take the perfect/imperfect sequence (as in v. 19c, 'they sought food to revive their strength') as indicating a final clause: 'you have brought the day which you announced so that they should be as I was'. The thought is again one of reversal. The enemies now occupy the position which Jerusalem once had, perhaps in terms of pre-eminence (cf. vv. 1, 5), or even in terms of divine favour. Whereas the city had always thought itself chosen by God, and had regarded judgement as something which happened only to her enemies, it now appears that God's wrath has turned against her, while her enemies remain unscathed.

22. The final verse seeks a remedy to this situation. Justice demands that God should **deal with them** as he has dealt with Zion (cf. the same root in v. 12: 'my sorrow which was *brought upon me*'), because they are also guilty of **evil doing**. The implication of the third line, **for my groans are many and my heart is faint**, may be either that such action by God will give the victim some relief from her distress (it will perhaps remove oppression by the enemies, or change their attitude, or at least make Zion feel better); or that her distress should move God to act. Heb. *kî* (**for**) may, of course, simply be emphatic (as in *JB* and *NIV*), although this does not make much difference to the interpretative possibilities.

SWALLOWED UP IN ANGER 2:1-22

The second poem, like the first, contains the words of two speakers, the narrator and Zion, although the former has much more to say on this occasion than the latter. His words occupy the first nineteen verses: she speaks only in the closing three. His contribution comprises two addresses, one to the reader (vv. 1–12) and one to Zion herself (vv. 13–19). In the former, as in chapter 1 (vv.1–11), a calamity which has befallen Jerusalem is described. The tenor of the address to the reader in this second poem is, however, quite different from that in the first. There the emphasis falls upon *what has happened* to Zion: it is her piteous state which is uppermost in the author's mind. The first poem begins, therefore, 'How lonely sits the city that was full of people . . .' (1:1), and most of the material in the following ten verses is concerned to fill out this picture of desolation. God is mentioned as the *cause* of what has happened only once (1:5). Here, however, the emphasis falls as much upon the *cause* of the calamity as upon the events themselves. The second poem, therefore, begins 'How the Lord in his anger has set the daughter of Zion under a cloud . . .', and the following seven verses continue this theme. Virtually no other actor but God is, in fact, mentioned in the first eight verses of the poem. He dominates the scene entirely with his anger (vv. 1, 2, 3, 4, 6) and destructiveness (vv. 2, 3, 5, 6, 7, 8). The latter is most often expressed by the keyword *billa'*, 'to swallow up', which occurs four times in these verses (vv. 2, 5 [twice], 8) and once later in the chapter (v. 16), but nowhere else in the book. It is only with vv. 9–12 that the divine causality again retreats (temporarily) into the background and we are given a simple description of Jerusalem's state. The emotional outburst which this provokes (vv. 11–12) leads on to the narrator's second, impassioned address, directed to Zion (vv. 13–19). He reiterates to her that the disaster is God's doing—her enemies may have 'swallowed her up' (v. 16), but it was God who was acting in their actions (v. 17)—and on this ground exhorts her to pray for relief (vv. 18–19). Zion's address to God in response to this exhortation follows in vv. 20–22.

As in the first poem, there is no disagreement between the narrator and Zion as to the causes of suffering: her speech makes clear that she accepts his basic thesis, that God is indeed the source of her troubles. We again receive hints, however, that there is not complete unanimity between them in their responses to this fact. The first poem ended, it will be recalled, with a suggestion of Zion's dissatisfaction with the narrator's seemingly simple equation between suffering and sin. Whereas there was no trace of doubt in his words as to the justice of the divine action in history, she felt that she was no worse than her enemies, and that it was unjust that she should suffer while they did not. In the second poem, the justice of God is again not an issue to the narrator. It is simply assumed that the calamity is sufficiently explained by Zion's 'iniquity', and that the only proper response comprises prayer and (implicitly) confession of sin, in the hope that her fortunes will be restored (cf. v. 14). It is interesting to note, however, that while Zion does seek God's compassion in the midst of her misery, confession of sin forms no part of her address to him (vv. 20–22). Indeed, there is the suggestion of a reproach in her voice. The punishment is greater than that endured by others, or perhaps greater than those punished deserved (see the comment on v. 20). As in the first poem, then, a hint of the *problem* of suffering for the religious believer—the questions it poses with regard to the goodness and omnipotence of God—is apparent in Zion's words which is not present in the words of the narrator. No resolution to this problem, like that offered in 1:21–22, is suggested here, and no clear hope of any resolution is apparent. It is not clear whether either Zion or the narrator (whose implicit hope of v. 14 must be balanced against his explicit despair of v. 13) really expect her lot to improve or not.

For a general discussion of the historical circumstances in which this second lament might have been written, see 'Author, Date and Place of Composition' in the Introduction.

*

1. How the Lord in his anger has set the daughter of Zion under a cloud: the verb *yāʿîb*, which *RSV* translates **set . . . under**

a cloud, occurs only here in the *OT* and is of uncertain meaning. Translators both ancient and modern, like *RSV*, have generally connected it with the noun *ʿāb*, 'cloud, thicket', though differing in their precise rendering of the line (cf., for example, *NEB*'s 'What darkness the Lord in his anger has brought . . .'). This explanation of the verb may well be correct. If it is, then we could understand the line as deliberately contrasting past blessings with the present calamity in the same way as the first poem often does. Elsewhere in the *OT* (e.g. Exod. 19:9, 34:5–6; I Kg. 8:10–13), God's contact with Israel through the medium of a cloud is usually something positive. Here it is negative: he 'overclouds' Zion in his wrath (Albrektson, *Studies*, 85–86). In the nature of the case, however, we cannot be sure that *yāʿîb* and *ʿāb* are indeed connected in this way. Some scholars (e.g. Rudolph, 218) have suggested on the basis of the Arabic root *ʿyb*, 'to blame, revile' that we should rather translate the line 'How the Lord in his anger has disgraced . . . Zion'; while others (e.g. McDaniel, 'Studies', 34–35; Brandscheidt, *Gotteszorn und Menschenleid*, 126) regard *yāʿîb* as related to the Heb. root *tʿb* and translate: 'How the Lord in his anger has made an abomination of . . . Zion/treated . . . Zion with contempt' (cf. the similar use of *tʿb* in Ps. 106:40). Targ.'s 'How has the LORD detested the congregation of Zion . . .' could be taken as supporting either of these suggestions.

A degree of uncertainty also exists with regard to the interpretation of the remainder of the verse, centring on the precise meaning of both **splendour of Israel** and **his footstool**. It is, first of all, unclear whether Heb. *tipʾārāh* (*RSV*'s **splendour**) refers here to an attribute possessed by Israel (i.e. the line describes the fall of the *nation* from her exalted position), or to some concrete possession of hers. If the latter is intended, there are several possibilities: the city of Jerusalem (cf. the closely analogous Isa. 13:19, 'Babylon . . . the splendour . . . of the Chaldeans'); the king (cf. other *OT* references to the fall of rulers from positions of pre-eminence, such as Isa. 14:3–21 and Ezek. 28:11–19); the temple; or even more specifically, the ark of the covenant. The last of these comes to mind because God's **footstool**, secondly, is

certainly the ark in I Chr. 28:2 and may be so in other instances
also (Ps. 99:5, 132:7). Of course, it may refer more widely in these
places, as also here, to the temple (cf. Targ., *JB*'s footnote and
'the place of the soles of my feet' in Ezek. 43:7) or even to Jerusalem
as a whole (cf. *NEB*'s very free 'did not remember . . . that Zion
was his footstool'). We cannot be entirely sure (*contra* Albrektson,
Studies, 85–86).

The details of the verse are not certain, then. Its general thrust,
however, is clear enough. God has turned against his people,
ignoring their special status (**he has not remembered his footstool**),
and has removed them from their position of pre-eminence (**He
has cast down from heaven to earth**). The motivation behind this
action is **anger**. This is given particular emphasis here through the
presence of Heb. *'appô*, **his anger**, at both the beginning and end
of the verse, framing the remainder of the content. It is in the
context of God's anger that everything else is to be understood.
The scene is thus set for the immediately following verses, which
elaborate upon God's anger and its consequences for Israel.

2. The Lord has destroyed . . . all the habitations of Jacob:
RSV's **destroyed** is a rather colourless translation of Heb. *billa'*,
which occurs also in 2:5, 8, 16 and is a keyword of this chapter. The
same verbal root is used elsewhere to mean 'to swallow up' (e.g. in
the case of Jonah and the fish, Jon. 1:17 [MT 2:1]), and such a
rendering would also be appropriate here (cf. *AV* and *NIV*). Heb.
nᵉ'ôt is, moreover, better translated 'pastures' than **habitations** or
'beautiful things' (LXX, Targ.). The latter interpretation is unlikely
to be correct both because the context does not favour it and because
nᵉ'ôt is always elsewhere the construct plural of the noun *nāwāh*
rather than of the adjective *nā'weh*, 'beautiful, seemly'; while the
other occurrences of *nᵉ'ôt* in the *OT* (cf. Jer. 9:10 [MT 9:9]; 23:10;
25:37; Jl 1:19, 20; 2:22; Am. 1:2; Ps. 23:2; 65:12 [MT 65:13]; 74:20;
83:12 [MT 83:13]) provide no clear support for the meaning
habitations. The line is best translated, then: 'The Lord has
swallowed up . . . all the pastures of Jacob', referring to the land
in general. More specifically, **he has broken down the
strongholds . . .**, the fortified cities of the land.

he has brought down to the ground in dishonour the kingdom and its rulers: LXX has '. . . her *king(s)* and her rulers' (cf. also Syr.). Whether this reflects a different Heb. text, perhaps reading *malkāh wᵉśāreyhā* (found also in 2:9) or *mᵉlākeyhā wᵉśāreyhā* instead of MT's *mamlākāh wᵉśāreyhā*, or is simply a loose translation of MT, is unclear. A few scholars have followed W. F. Albright ('The Oracles of Balaam', *JBL* 63 (1944) 207–233, on p. 218, n. 70; *idem*, 'A Catalogue of Early Hebrew Lyric Poems (Psalm lxviii)', *HUCA* 23/1 (1950–1951) 1–39, on p. 34) in arguing, on the basis of Ugaritic *mmlkt*, that *mamlākāh* can itself mean 'king'. This, too, is uncertain. Gottlieb, *Study*, 24–25, has rightly pointed out both that such an understanding of the word is nowhere required elsewhere in the *OT*, and that its adoption here creates a difficulty with regard to the suffix on *wᵉśāreyhā*: 'he has brought down . . . the king and *her* rulers'. Between MT and LXX, however, there is no way of deciding: both make perfectly good sense in the context.

3. He has cut down in fierce anger all the might of Israel: lit. '. . . all the/every horn of Israel'. To have one's 'horn' exalted by God was to be given power or honour by him (2:17; I Sam. 2:10; Ps. 112:9). To exalt one's own 'horn' was to trespass on God's prerogative and thus to behave arrogantly (Ps. 75: 4–5 [MT 75:5–6]). The opposite of 'exaltation' in this context is Heb. *gdʿ*, **cut down** or 'cut off' (Ps. 75:10 [MT 75:11]). The imagery seems to depend upon a contrast between the wild ox, which is able to hold its horned head proud and erect in a lordly fashion, and the domestic ox, burdened with its yoke and perhaps with its horns clipped (cf. Ps. 92:10 [MT 92:11]). The line may mean, then (as *RSV* has it), simply that God in a general way has rendered Israel powerless. **he has withdrawn from them his right hand** in the second line of the verse certainly means this (cf. also the yoke imagery in 1:14, which refers to the same, and Jer. 48:25, 'The horn of Moab is cut off, and his arm is broken . . .'). Alternatively, it may mean that he has humbled her (cf. *NEB*'s '. . . he hacked down the horn of Israel's pride'). The horn also stands in the *OT* as a symbol for particular individuals or entities who are powerful, however: a king of the Davidic line in Ps. 132:17, for example;

God in 2 Sam. 22:3 and Ps. 18:2 [MT 18:3]; a deliverer of uncertain identity in Ps. 148:14; foreign kings or kingdoms in Zech. 1:18–21 [MT 2:1–4] and Dan. 7:8 ff. The meaning may, therefore, be that 'God has cut off every horn, i.e. every source of power or deliverance, in Israel', of which the strongholds and rulers of the previous verse are particular examples.

he has burned like a flaming fire: in the Exodus narratives **fire**, like cloud (cf. v.1), is a symbol of God's presence with Israel for blessing (e.g. Exod. 13:21–22). God's **right hand** is also very much in evidence in those narratives, operating on Israel's behalf (Exod. 15:6, 12). Now his **right hand** is no longer with them, and the **fire**, like the cloud, symbolizes only his wrath. Truly God has turned against them!

4. He has bent his bow like an enemy, with his right hand set like a foe: *RSV* includes Heb. $k^e\bar{s}\bar{a}r$, **like a foe**, in the first line (with MT, which is supported by the Versions), and understands $y^e m\hat{i}n\hat{o}$, **his right hand**, as the subject of the verb $ni\bar{s}\bar{s}\bar{a}b$, **set**. Many scholars have objected to this reading of $k^e\bar{s}\bar{a}r$, on the ground that its inclusion as part of the first line means that one of the succeeding lines (depending upon where one divides these) is much shorter than the other two. Among the many solutions to this problem which have been proposed, the most popular is that $k^e\bar{s}\bar{a}r$ should be separated from $ni\bar{s}\bar{s}\bar{a}b$ $y^e m\hat{i}n\hat{o}$, and thus removed from the first line, and be taken instead with the following $wayyah^a r\bar{o}g$, **and he has slain** (cf. the division of the verse in *BHS*). This is dubious procedure, however, in view of the limitations of our knowledge concerning Hebrew poetry (cf. 'Text and Interpretation' in the Introduction). Moreover, it immediately involves us in conjectural emendation (cf., for example, Rudolph, 219, who reads $k^e\bar{s}\bar{a}r$ after $wayyah^a r\bar{o}g$ rather than before it; Hillers, 31, 37, who adds another verb before $wayyah^a r\bar{o}g$; and Albrektson, *Studies*, 92, who reads $b\bar{a}\bar{s}ar$ for $k^e\bar{s}\bar{a}r$), since $k^e\bar{s}\bar{a}r$ $wayyah^a r\bar{o}g$, 'like a foe and he has slain', is not likely to be the original reading. It is much the preferable course of action to retain MT, which provides us with a nicely balanced and perfectly comprehensible line. *RSV*'s interpretation of it is, however, perhaps not the most likely, since it requires that the feminine noun *yāmîn* govern the masculine verb *niṣṣāb*. While difference in gender between a noun and its verb is not unknown in Heb. (cf. GKC §145), a precise parallel to the example here does not appear to exist. It is probably better, therefore, to understand the subject of *niṣṣāb* as 'God'. We might then translate 'standing there with hostile right hand' (cf. Gordis, 161) or, taking a lead from *JB*, 'holding his hostile right hand steady', taking the phrase as a reference to the archer who is on the point of shooting. The *hiṣṣîb* (for *niṣṣāb*) which may be implied by LXX and Syr. (but see Gottlieb, *Study*, 26) could also be understood in this way. As in the previous verse, the point is that Yahweh's protection has turned to hostility. He has used his **right hand** to bend **his bow like an enemy**.

he has slain all the pride of our eyes: it is not explicitly stated in the text to whom the eyes belong, and the phrase has sometimes therefore been translated as if it referred to physical appearance (cf. *NIV*'s 'all who were pleasing to the eye'; Hillers, 31, 37, has 'all the good-looking men'!). This seems rather implausible. Heb. *maḥmad*, **pride**, appears also in 1:10, and the closely related *maḥmôd* in 1:7, 11. In these verses the translation 'precious things' or 'precious ones' was offered, and it is best to render *maḥmad* here in the same way: 'all that was precious'. To whom these people were precious is then a matter of interpretation—the people represented by the narrator (cf. *RSV*'s 'our'); Zion (perhaps implied by LXX, cf. comment on 1:10); or God himself (cf. *NEB*'s 'all those who had been his delight')?

in the tent of the daughter of Zion: this phrase could equally well be taken with what precedes it (as the place where God slew the people: so *RSV*) or with what follows it (as the place where, or upon which, **God poured out his fury like fire:** so *NEB*). **the tent** probably refers to Judah or Jerusalem as 'daughter Zion's' dwelling, rather than to the Temple or the army camp (cf. Kraus, 43).

5. The Lord has become like an enemy, he has destroyed Israel: the claims that God is now behaving towards Israel **like an enemy** and that he has 'swallowed her up' (Heb. *billaʿ*, cf.

comment on v. 2) are repeated and thus emphasized. The **strongholds** are also mentioned again (cf. v. 2), this time along with the **palaces** (or perhaps 'citadels'), whose unexpected feminine suffix (lit. 'her palaces', in contrast to 'his strongholds') is probably to be explained (with Kraus, 37, and Albrektson, *Studies*, 93) as due to the influence of 'daughter of Zion' in v. 4. As in v. 7, the **palaces** are specifically those of Zion, the **strongholds** those of Israel more generally. God's action against his people has **multiplied . . . mourning and lamentation** (Heb. *taʾᵃnîyyāh waʾᵃnîyyāh*), perhaps better translated 'mourning and moaning' (so Meek, 18) in order to bring out the play on words.

6. He has broken down his booth like that of a garden, laid in ruins the place of his appointed feasts: MT (Heb. *wayyaḥmōs kaggan śukkô šiḥēt môʿᵃdô*) is very difficult here, and *RSV*'s translation assumes at least two things about it. First, it assumes that *môʿᵃdô* refers to a *location*, **the place of his appointed feasts**; and secondly, that *śōk* (which occurs only here in the *OT*) is a variant of *sōk* (which actually appears here in several Heb. mss.), and refers, like *sōk* in Ps. 27:5, 76:2 [MT 76:3], to God's dwelling, **his booth**. The first assumption may certainly be questioned. Heb. *môʿēd* appears also in the second line, where it most probably refers to a festival or festivals (cf. *RSV*'s **appointed feast**), rather than to the place in which they took place. As Peake, 316, notes, it would be a little strange if the same word were used in successive lines with different meanings. It is better, then, to translate *môʿēd* in the first line also as 'festival' ('he has ruined his festival': cf. also LXX, Syr.). The first line of the verse refers to a particular festival which was disrupted by God's action, the second to the effect of this action on cultic celebration generally. The second assumption, about the meaning of *śōk*, is in itself not unreasonable. The problem lies not so much with *śōk* taken in isolation, as with its occurrence alongside *kaggan*.

The difficulty with *kaggan*, 'like a garden', is to know what exactly it means in the context. If *śōk* is indeed related to *sōk* and *sukkāh*, and is therefore to be taken as a rough and temporary shelter such as was erected, for example, for those guarding crops (Isa. 1:8; Job

27:18), the comparison might be between two such dwellings, as *RSV* has it. The idea could be that God has destroyed his dwelling *as easily* as one might destroy such a shelter (so Meek, 18; Albrektson, *Studies*, 95–96). *kaggan* then means 'as one would to a booth in a garden'. The comparison might, on the other hand, be between the dwelling and the garden, rather than between two dwellings: 'he has wrecked his own domain like a garden' (*JB*). The reference might again be to the ease with which the deed was done ('as if it were a garden'), assuming that it requires comparatively little effort to destroy a garden. We might even take *kaggan* as referring to the consequence of the action: 'he has treated his dwelling so violently that it has become like a garden', i.e. the site has been levelled and is devoid of habitation. One does have to work quite hard, however, to make sense of the word. It is interesting, therefore, that LXX ('he has spread out his tabernacle as a vine') appears to presuppose, instead of *kaggan*, a Heb. *kᵉgepen*, 'like a vine'. Confusion in the consonantal text between *kgn* and *kgpn* is, of course, quite conceivable (cf. McDaniel, 'Studies', 37). *NEB* follows this lead, rendering the line 'he stripped his tabernacle as a vine is stripped'. McDaniel ('Studies', 36–38) argues that *śōk* should be understood, not as booth, but as 'branch' (cf. *śōk* in Jg. 9:49). Emending the preposition before *gepen*, he translates 'he has stripped from the vine its branches'. One wonders, however, whether such translations pay sufficient attention to the only other occasion upon which the relatively rare verb *ḥāmas* appears along with *gepen*. Job 15:33 begins thus: *yaḥmōs kaggepen bisrô*—'he will shake off, like the vine, his unripe grapes'. Here the vine is represented as taking vigorous, even violent action against its own fruit. The text which probably lies behind LXX, then (*wayyaḥmōs kᵉgepen śukkô*: see Albrektson, *Studies*, 94, 96–97, for a discussion of LXX with regard to the first and last words), might better be translated, 'He has cut off, like a vine, his branch'. God is depicted as a vine which carries out its own pruning, and Zion as the branch which had depended upon him for sustenance and is now separated from him. It was, of course, unfruitful branches in particular which were pruned from vines (cf. Jn. 15:1–7), and the image of Israel herself as an unfruitful vine, incurring God's wrath, occurs elsewhere in the OT (cf. Isa. 5:1–7).

Which festival does the author have in mind? On either reading of the first part of the line, it seems likely that it is the feast of Tabernacles or Booths. The images of the **booth** and the vine both point in this direction, since the people lived in 'booths' (Heb. *sukkôt*) made of branches during this festival (Lev. 23:42–43), and it followed 'the ingathering from your threshing floor and your wine press' (Dt. 16:13). The point of the line is that God has ruined this occasion for rejoicing by destroying *his* **booth**/cutting off his branch, that is the temple/Zion, the focal point of the celebrations.

the LORD has brought to an end in Zion appointed feast and sabbath: the Piel of the Heb. root *škḥ* (*RSV*'s **has brought to an end**) occurs only here in the *OT*, and its precise nuance is therefore unclear. In the Qal it means 'to forget, cease to care about' (e.g. Lam. 5:20). It may also have this meaning here ('the Lord has ceased to care about feast and sabbath in Zion': cf. LXX, which may, however, have read a Qal), although it is most often thought to have a causative sense: 'the Lord has caused to forget/be forgotten'. *RSV* understands this to imply that God has abolished **feast and sabbath** in the city, an implication also seen by Targ., which offers the paraphrase 'the Lord . . . *the enjoyment* of feast and sabbath' in order to avoid it. Even if the verb is a causative, however, abolition is not necessarily in view, nor even the long-term suspension envisaged by *JB* ('wiped out the memory of festivals and sabbaths') and *NEB* ('blotted out all memory of festal assembly and of sabbath'). All that may be meant is that observation of these religious institutions has lapsed in the context of the immediate crisis described. The inhabitants of the city have other things on their minds as a result of God's actions against them. A specific reason for this situation is that **king and priest** (LXX reads 'king, priest and prince') have been rejected, which probably implies 'removed' (cf. v. 9). They cannot therefore carry out their cultic functions. It is possible that the singular **priest** refers to the chief priest (Targ., cf. 2 Kg. 25:18 f. and Kraus, 44), but more probable that, on the analogy of the singular nouns in the second line (**appointed feast and sabbath**), it refers to priests in general.

7. God's action against the cult is further described. He has **scorned** (better 'rejected', *NIV*) **his altar** and **disowned his sanctuary**. Moreover, **he has delivered into** (LXX 'broken by') **the hand of the enemy the walls of her palaces** (or 'citadels'). The feminine suffix (**her palaces**) presumably refers back to the 'Zion' of the previous verse, since **sanctuary** is a masculine noun (cf. a similar situation with the same word in v. 5). This line is, therefore, in spite of the support which MT receives from the Versions, often held to be corrupt (e.g. by Rudolph, 219), since it is argued that a reference to Zion's **palaces** is out of place in a context which concerns the temple. Whether we may demand such precision when city and temple were so closely identified is questionable, as Albrektson, *Studies*, 100, rightly points out.

a clamour was raised: *NIV*'s 'they have raised a shout' (cf. also *AV, NEB*) makes clearer what is meant here. **the enemy**, having gained access to the temple, engaged in boisterous celebration of the kind normally associated in Israel with **the day of an appointed feast** (Heb. *yôm mô'ēd*). *mô'ēd* twice appears in v. 6, of course, in the context of the description of the disruption caused to Israel's worship by God's actions against her. Its use here is therefore quite striking. God has enabled Israel's enemies to engage in a parody of this worship in the very temple itself!

8. Attention now turns to the wall of the city, which God had **determined** (LXX 'turned', perhaps reading a Heb. *hēsīb* for MT's *hāšab*) to destroy. In preparation for this, **he marked it off by the line** (Heb. *nāṭāh qāw*, better translated with *NIV* 'he stretched out a measuring line'). The same phrase is used on several occasions elsewhere in the OT of the preparations for *building* work (cf. Isa. 44:13; Zech. 1:16; Job 38:5), and several scholars have found it puzzling that here and in 2 Kg. 21:13, Isa. 34:11 (cf. also Isa. 28:17) it can also be employed in the context of destruction. To quote Hillers, 38: 'It is not completely clear how a phrase from the vocabulary of building becomes a synonym for destruction . . .'. It is possible, however, to imagine situations other than the construction of buildings in which a measuring line, and the other tools of measurement which are associated with it, such as the *mišqōlet*, 'levelling instrument' (2 Kg. 21:13, Isa. 28:17), and *ʾeben*, 'plummet' (Isa. 34:11), might have been used. Demolition itself requires careful planning (Kaiser, 336), and measurements are also needed when buildings are surveyed in order to find out if they need to be demolished. The metaphorical use of *nāṭāh qāw* here could easily be understood against such a background. God first checks the wall and condemns it. Only then does he proceed to destroy it.

he restrained not his hand from destroying: lit. 'he did not bring back his hand from swallowing up', the latter verb being the same (*billaʿ*) as in vv. 2, 5. The consequence is that both **rampart and wall . . . lament: they languish together**, or 'together lay dejected' (*NEB*). *JB* understands the second verb as describing a physical occurrence ('crumbling down together') rather than an attitude, and it is indeed possible that this idea is also present. We find a similar double reference in the first line of the next verse. LXX and Syr. divide the final line differently, but with little difference in meaning.

9. Her gates have sunk into the ground; he has ruined and broken her bars: Heb. *ṭābaʿ*, **sunk**, is used metaphorically in Ps. 69:2, 14 [MT 69:3, 15] of a person in distress, who is said to have 'sunk in the mire'. We might suppose, then, that an element of personification is to be found in the choice of the verb here. As the 'ramparts and walls' of the previous verse 'lament', so the gates also are in distress. At the same time there can be little doubt, given the context of broken wall (v. 8) and **bars**, that the author also intends to tell us that the **gates** were in reality severely damaged. Apart from walls, **gates** and **bars** were the characteristic fortifications of cities in the *OT* (Dt. 3:5; I Sam. 23:7; 2 Chr. 8:5), and their mention together here emphasizes the completeness of the devastation of Jerusalem's defences. This is also emphasized by the use of the two verbs of similar meaning ('destroyed and shattered') before **her bars**.

her king and princes are among the nations; the law is no more: God's action against the political leaders of the community

(cf. the comment on **princes** in 1:6) has already been referred to
in general terms in vv. 2 and 6. Here for the first time, however,
we have specific mention of their exile: they are **among the nations**.
The relation of the latter part of the line (Heb. *ʾên tôrāh*, lit. 'there
is/was not law/instruction) to this is not entirely clear. The
accentuation of MT suggests that *ʾên tôrāh* actually refers to the
state of **the nations**: 'among the nations who have no law', i.e.
among heathen nations. Targ., on the other hand, takes the absence
of law(-keeping) to be the *reason* for exile. God has so dealt with
Israel because they did not keep the law. We might also view the
absence of law as the *consequence* of the exile of **king** and **princes**.
Without the presence of the mediators of the law, there can *be* no
law. The most popular interpretation of the phrase, however, and
the one which seems most plausible, is to take it as one of three
separate clauses referring to important groups in Israel. Specifically
referred to are political rulers and **prophets**; while in *ʾên tôrāh* we
have an allusion to the priests, who are no longer offering priestly
instruction (cf. Jer. 18:18; Ezek. 7:26 for *tôrāh* in this sense: Mic.
3:11 is also relevant). Whether this is because they have been
removed along with the rulers (v. 6 may imply that king and priests
suffered the same fate) or for some other reason is not made clear.
The **prophets** seem clearly to be still resident in Jerusalem (see
the comment on v. 14), but they too have ceased to function as
channels of God's guidance. They **obtain no vision from the
LORD**, which in the light of v. 14 seems to mean that **the LORD**
has ceased to speak through them rather than that they have stopped
prophesying altogether. The people have evidently lost not only
their temporal authorities, then, but also whatever access they had
to the realm of the divine. They receive no guidance from God,
neither through priestly pronouncement nor prophetic **vision**. The
order and structure of society has broken down.

**10. The elders of the daughter of Zion sit on the ground in
silence:** lit. '. . . sit on the ground, are silent' (Heb. *yēšᵉbû lāʾāreṣ
yiddᵉmû*). Sitting **on the ground**, putting **dust** on one's **head** and
clothing oneself in sackcloth were all elements of traditional
mourning ritual (cf. Jos. 7:6; Ezek. 27:28–31; and especially Job

2:12–13). Whether the observance of **silence** was also such is a matter of dispute (cf. N. Lohfink, 'Enthielten die im Alten Testament bezeugten Klageriten eine Phase des Schweigens?', *VT* 12 (1962) 260–277). Partly because of doubts about this, several scholars (e.g. McDaniel, 'Studies', 38–39; cf. *NEB*) prefer to render the verb *yiddˤmû* as 'they wail, mourn', a meaning which the root *dmm* does appear to have in Isa. 23:2. Even if the keeping of silence was not a ritual act, however, the context still favours the traditional rendering of the first line. **The elders** were, like the rulers, priests and prophets, important people in Israelite society. They provided advice and guidance, and participated in decision-making (as in I Kg. 12:6–7). The reference to their **silence**, then, may be understood in the light of the previous verse. Like those others who provided leadership and dispensed wisdom, they have nothing to say. They are fully occupied with their grieving.

the maidens of Jerusalem have bowed their heads to the ground: the bowing of the head was another sign of self-abasement and humiliation (cf. Isa. 58:5; Job 10:15), here associated with mourning.

11–12. Hitherto the narrator's feelings about the events have been veiled behind his description of them. From this point on, however, his emotional involvement becomes clear. He is plainly someone very much caught up in the tragedy.

My eyes are spent with weeping, lit. '. . . are at an end on account of tears' (Heb. *kālû baddˤmāʿôt*). This could mean that crying has worn his eyes out (cf. *kālāh* in 4:17 and Ps. 69:3 [MT 69:4]; 119:82, 123) or that tears are presently obstructing his sight (cf. *NEB*'s 'my eyes are blinded with tears').

my soul is in tumult: lit. 'my stomach (Heb. *mēʿîm*) is in tumult', a phrase already discussed above (see the comment on 1:20). The stomach is often referred to as a seat of the emotions in the *OT*, and to say that it is **in tumult** is to say that the emotions are in turmoil.

my heart is poured out in grief: lit. 'my liver (Heb. *kābēd*) is poured out onto the ground'. *NEB* ('my bile is spilt on the earth') takes this as a description of a physical occurrence. Bile is, of course, a product of the liver. The context suggests, however, that *RSV* is closer to the mark in taking the 'liver' here, like the 'stomach' of the first line, as an emotional centre. Interestingly, although such a view of this organ is found in other ancient Semitic writings, and the idea is consistent with what we know about Heb. anthropology in general (see H. W. Wolff, *Anthropology of the Old Testament*, London, 1974, 63–66), MT contains no other reference to the liver in this sense. It has long been suspected, however, that *kābēd*, 'liver', has on some occasions been confused, in the course of the transmission of the text, with *kābôd*, 'glory', a noun from the same root. This very confusion is apparent, indeed, in the LXX and Syr. of the present verse, where both read 'my glory' instead of 'my liver'. It is therefore possible that the liver originally appeared more often in the *OT* than it does now. Ps. 16:9, 30:12 [MT 30:13], 57:8 [MT 57:9] and 108:1 [MT 108:2], where the *kābôd* is described as rejoicing and praising, strike one as places where this might be so, since the parallelism of the verses implies it, and these very functions are ascribed to the liver in Akkadian documents. What the whole phrase here in 2:11 might signify is best indicated by the other occasions upon which organs thought of as a seat of the emotions are said to have been **poured out** (Heb. root *špk*), particularly in the present chapter (see the comment immediately below and that on v.19). Certainly it refers to the poet's deep distress (cf. Job 30:16). It may well also refer to his prayers to God on behalf of the people (cf. I Sam. 1:15, Ps. 62:8 [MT 62:9]).

infants and babes faint in the streets of the city (or better, 'city squares'): the specific cause of the author's distress, to the description of which the whole of v. 12 is also given over, is the plight of the children of Jerusalem in the aftermath of the terrible events related in vv. 1–10. They **faint** (Heb. *ʿṭp*) through weakness because of hunger and thirst, crying out **to their mothers** for sustenance. *RSV* seems to interpret the final line of v. 12 to mean that they actually die: **their life** (Heb. *nepeš*, which is often translated 'soul') **is poured out on their mothers' bosom**. The death of children is indeed implied elsewhere in the poem (v. 20), but the other occasions upon which *nepeš* occurs alongside *špk* suggest that it is not so much death as suffering which is in view at this point. When a person is 'pouring out the soul', (s)he is experiencing extreme distress (Job 30:16) and perhaps communicating this distress to another (I Sam. 1:15, Ps. 42:4 [MT 42:5]). It is particularly noteworthy in this context that the heading to Ps. 102 [MT 102:1] reads: 'A prayer of one afflicted, when he is faint (Heb. *ya'ᵃṭōp*) and pours out (Heb. *yišpōk*) his complaint before the Lord'. 'Fainting' and complaining go together here. It seems probable, then, that the reference is not just to the suffering of the children as they lie in their mothers' arms, but also to their cries for food of which we have been told in the first line.

13. What can I say for you . . .?: there has been much debate about the meaning of the verb (Heb. *ᵃ'īdēk*, from *'wd*) in this phrase. *RSV* apparently follows the lead of LXX and Syr. in taking *'wd* in its common sense of 'to bear witness, testify' ('what can I say on your behalf?'), with the implication that such support will be of some comfort (cf. Job 29:11 for a similar usage—the eye 'speaking approvingly' of Job's deeds). The first two lines of the verse as it is in MT (but see below) then fit together quite neatly in a chiastic structure: **What can I say** to you for your comfort, **to what compare you . . . What can I liken to you, that I may comfort you . . .?** A similar construction is obtained if we follow the suggestion of Gordis, 164, and take *'wd* here, in the light of its use in Ps. 20:8 [MT 20:9], 146:9, as referring to the lifting up and support of the downtrodden and oppressed. Such an understanding of the verb is found in some Targ. mss. We might then translate: 'How may I build you up . . . **that I may comfort you?**' Another possibility, however, is that the first and second lines are not parallel, and that both verbs in the former mean roughly the same. Ehrlich, *Randglossen*, 37, noting Jer. 49:19, suggests that *ᵃ'īdēk* in Lam 2:13 is synonymous with the following *ᵃdammeh-lāk*: 'To what may I liken you, **to what compare you . . .?**' This is the way in which Vulg. renders the line, and is perhaps the most satisfactory of all the possibilities.

What can I liken to you, that I may comfort you, O virgin daughter of Zion?: MT is usually interpreted as meaning that the poet is searching for an historical analogy to Zion's downfall. If such could be found, then she might find comfort in knowing that her plight was not unique, and perhaps in being aware that destruction was often not the end of the story. The final line of the verse, however, suggests that it may rather be a simile from the realm of nature—no doubt something which also implies restoration after great destruction—which is being sought. The task is beyond him, however: the calamity is too great. The only simile which comes to mind is the vastness of the **sea**, and this induces despair rather than hope. It is impossible to see how anyone might **restore** the city in the context of such great **ruin** (Heb. *šeber*, rendered 'destruction' in v.11: note the clever play on words here, emphasized by Targ., since Heb. *mišbār* from the same root means 'breaker, wave'). The author's attempt at being the comforter whose absence was so often lamented in chapter 1 is thus unsuccessful. LXX also communicates this despair (though apparently reading Heb. *kôs*, 'cup', for *kayyām*, **as the sea**: 'the cup of your destruction is enlarged'), but reads the second line thus: 'who shall save and comfort you, O virgin daughter of Zion?' (cf. *JB*). This removes the close connection between the first two lines: MT certainly seems the more satisfactory text.

14. Your prophets have seen for you false and deceptive visions: lit. '. . . emptiness and tasteless things' or '. . . emptiness and whitewash'. There are two Heb. words *tāpēl*, and it is not entirely clear which is intended here. The association of whitewash with false prophecy in Ezek. 13:8–16, however, tends to suggest that it is the latter. The prophecies of these **prophets** have lacked substance and, like whitewash on a badly built or deteriorating wall, have served only to conceal the true nature of the situation. Their **oracles** have been **false and misleading**, lit. 'emptiness and seduction'. The latter word, which occurs only here in the *OT*, could also be rendered 'banishment' (cf. LXX, *AV, NEB* footnote): 'oracles which result in banishment'. The prophets have thus failed in their duty of exposing **iniquity**. Had they fulfilled their duty, Zion's **fortunes** now might be quite different, presumably because knowledge of iniquity might have led to repentance (cf. Syr.). *JB*

('to ward off your exile') and *NIV* ('to ward off your captivity')
understand the reference here as only to the activity of prophets
before the disaster fell: true prophecy would have averted it. Both
the context and the usage elsewhere of the phrase *šûb/hēšîb*
šᵉbît/šᵉbût (note the Kethib/Qere), however, rather suggest that *RSV*
is correct in taking the verse as concerning false prophecy in the
present and as speaking of *restoration* of fortune (cf., for example,
Jer. 31:23, 32:44, Job 42:10). The lack of a 'vision from the LORD'
(v. 9) has been a crucial factor in perpetuating the dire situation
in which Zion has found herself ever since the events described
began. It is for this reason that the **prophets** are singled out in
v. 14. The author has noted in v. 13 that in reality there is nothing
comforting to be said about the situation, and he has posed the
question: 'Who can restore (lit. 'heal') you?'. The **prophets** come
to mind in this context because they should have been offering a
means of restoration but have failed to do so. They have offered
comfort where condemnation for sin and exhortation to repentance
were required.

15-16. Witnesses to the vastness of Zion's ruin include those
who pass by (**All who pass along the way**) and her **enemies**. The
former are commonly present in *OT* descriptions of lands or cities
upon which disaster has fallen (cf. 1:12; Jer. 18:13-17; 49:17-22;
50:11-16). When they see Jerusalem, they clap their hands (Heb.
sāpᵉqû kappayîm), an action which probably expresses hostility (cf.
Num. 24:10; Job 34:37). They also **hiss** or 'whistle' (Heb. *šāraq*),
an action which, like the 'wagging' (or 'shaking') of the **head** (cf.
2 Kg. 19:21; Ps. 22:7 [MT 22:8]) is often taken by translators (e.g.
NIV) and commentators to express contempt and derision. The
frequent appearance of this verb alongside Heb. *šāmam*, 'be
appalled, awestruck', however (cf. particularly Ezek. 27:35-36,
where the fear induced by disaster is emphasized), together with
its occurrence in Zeph. 2:15 alongside Heb. *hēnîʿa yād*, 'to shake
the fist', suggests rather that this too is an expression of hostility.
The passers-by are as pleased as the **enemies** to see Jerusalem,
regarded by the people of Israel as **the perfection** (LXX 'crown')
of beauty, the joy of all the earth (cf. Ps. 48:2 [MT 48:3]; 50:2),

cut down to size, and lose no time in letting their feelings be known. The **enemies**, for their part, 'open their mouths against' (*RSV*'s **rail against**) her, perhaps in order to taunt (cf. Job 16:10) or consume her (cf. Num. 16:30, and the 'swallowed her up' of the second line here), or perhaps simply to enable them to **hiss** and **gnash their teeth** (expressing either mockery, as in Ps. 35:16, or hostility, as in Ps. 112:10; Job 16:9). They have at last attained the goal they **longed for**. They have **destroyed her** (lit. 'swallowed her up', cf. vv. 2, 5, 8: *NEB*'s 'Here we are' in place of **We have destroyed her** has little justification or merit).

17. The LORD has done what he purposed, has carried out his threat: a restatement of the narrator's fundamental conviction, affirmed throughout vv. 1–8. It is God who has brought about the calamity. The **enemy** may think that it is they who have 'swallowed up' Zion, that this is their 'day' (v. 16). In reality, however, it is 'the day of *his* anger (v. 1)', long predicted by the prophets (e.g. Am. 5:18–20); and it is *he* (vv. 2, 5, 8) who has 'swallowed up' (so Hillers, 46). The **enemy** is only able to **rejoice** over Zion because God has **ordained it** so **long ago**. In their pitiless destruction of the city, it is he who **has demolished without pity** (v. 2). It is he who has **exalted the might** (lit. 'horn', which might also mean 'honour': cf. *NEB*) of the **foes**, while at the same time 'cutting down the might' of Israel (v. 3). Zion's enemies are but the players on the stage. It is God who directs the action.

18–19. Cry aloud to the Lord!: *RSV*, along with *JB, NEB* and most commentators, emend the text here. MT, which is supported by all the ancient Versions, reads 'Their heart cries out to the Lord' (cf. *NIV*). The subject in this case must be the inhabitants of Jerusalem, and the person addressed by the author must be, as (s)he was in vv. 1–12, the reader. The poet pauses in his address to Zion (vv. 13–19) to draw our attention to, and involve us in, her expression of her distress before God, before proceeding in the remainder of vv. 18–19 to encourage her in this activity. The second part of the first line in *RSV*, **O daughter of Zion!**, is also based on emendation. MT reads 'the/O wall of daughter Zion' (see the comment on 1:6 with regard to this translation), and is again substantially supported by the Versions (cf. Albrektson, *Studies*, 117–118). This might be taken with what follows in the second line ('O wall of daughter Zion, let tears stream down . . .'), the wall standing for Zion as a whole (a figure of speech known as synecdoche), as it is in LXX, Targ., *AV* and *NIV*. If it is taken in this way, it is more plausibly understood (*contra* LXX and *AV*) as the recommencement of the author's address to Zion than as the words of the people to Zion. It seems more probable, however, that it is a description of God: 'Their heart cries out to the Lord, the wall of daughter Zion' (so, for example, Gottwald, 11: cf. Zech. 2:5 [MT 2:9] for another occasion upon which God is described as Jerusalem's wall). The point is made throughout the poem, and has just been reiterated in v. 17, that it is God who is behind Zion's destruction. It is he who has destroyed the physical 'wall of daughter Zion' (v. 8). It is this fact which provides the basis for the exhortations to prayer in vv. 18–19. Because God is in control of these terrible events, it makes sense to intercede with him concerning them. That God himself should be described as 'the wall of daughter Zion' in this context is (*contra* Rudolph, 220) most natural. Those who pray approach him in the realization that it is only through him, and not by means of physical structures, that there can be real protection for Jerusalem.

The remainder of vv. 18–19 contains the author's exhortations to Zion to pray for relief from her distress. She is to weep without ceasing (cf. Jer. 14:17), to **cry out** even **in the night, at the beginning of the watches**. The night was divided into three watches (cf. Jg. 7:19; I Sam. 11:11), and in view of the context, **at the beginning of the watches** probably means 'at the beginning of every watch' (*NEB*; Rudolph, 226; Kaiser, 340) rather than 'at nightfall' (cf. *JB*'s 'in the early hours of darkness'). Indeed, we are probably to understand this as implying renewed effort at the commencement of each watch rather than a fresh start in prayer after sleep (cf. Ps. 63:6 [MT 63:7]). She must **give** herself **no rest** (Heb. *pûgat*: cf. the verb *pûg* in Ps. 77:2 [MT 77:3], also a context in which unrelenting prayer is described), her **eyes no respite** (lit. 'let not the daughter of your eye [i.e. pupil, Ps. 17:8] be still').

She is to **pour out her heart**, to tell God of her distress (cf. Ps. 62:8 [MT 62:9], and the comments on Heb. root *špk* in vv. 11–12); and she is to **lift her hands to him** in intercession for the **children** who are suffering so terribly from the famine (cf. vv. 11–12). The final line of v. 19 is often deleted by scholars (e.g. Brandscheidt, *Gotteszorn und Menschenleid*, 133) on the ground that it makes the verse much longer than the others in the poem. This is unjustified (cf. 'Text and Interpretation' in the Introduction, and the comment on 1:7).

20. In the final three verses of the poem, Zion herself addresses God. She further describes the terrible situation in which she finds herself, pleading that he would take notice of it (**Look, O LORD, and see!**: cf. the same phrase introducing Zion's speech in 1:11) and implicitly thereby asking that he would show compassion towards her. The reason why such compassion should be shown is given in the second part of the first line (**With whom hast thou dealt** (Heb. *'ôlaltā*, cf. 1:12, 22) **thus?**), although it is not clear from this whether the speaker has in mind the nature of the events or the nature of the people suffering. Is God to be compassionate because *Zion and her inhabitants* have suffered ('who is it that thou hast thus tormented?', *NEB*) or because they suffered so *severely* ('whom have you ever treated like this?', *JB, NIV*)? If the former is meant, then the point might either be that Zion and her inhabitants in a general sense, as the elect of God, should not have had to endure in such a way; or that the **women** and **children** (as the vulnerable of ancient society), priests and prophets (as God's agents in society) of this verse in particular should not have had to do so. The latter have been **slain** by the enemy (*contra* Targ., which implausibly takes the third line as an accusation against Zion from the mouth of God) **in the sanctuary of the Lord**—a particularly shocking place for this to have happened. The **women** have been driven by famine to **eat . . . the children of their tender care**. Heb. *ṭippuḥîm*, which *RSV* renders as **tender care**, occurs only here in the *OT* and is of uncertain meaning. The Heb. texts which lay before the translators of LXX and Syr. may, indeed, not have contained it (cf. Albrektson, *Studies*, 120–121). Syr. reads a verb, 'dashed in pieces', while LXX has the interesting double translation 'the cook has made a gleaning: shall the infants sucking at the breast be slain?' Targ., on the other hand, does appear to have read it and to have based its translation ('infants wrapped in swaddling-clothes') on the related Heb. *miṭpaḥat*, 'cloak'. *AV* ('children of a span long') follows Vulg., which takes its cue from the nouns *ṭepaḥ* and *ṭōpaḥ*, 'hand-breadth'. The idea that the reference is to the size of the children ('tiny children'?) is certainly possible. *ṭippuḥîm* is, however, probably best understood in the light of the use of the verb *ṭippaḥ* in v. 22 (*RSV*'s 'dandled'), where the context implies that it refers either to child-bearing or to the care of children in their earliest years (see below). *RSV* is therefore perhaps not precise enough in the present verse. *'ōlᵃlê ṭippuḥîm*, is better translated 'the children they have brought safely to birth' (*NEB*: cf. Kaiser, 328), or 'the children they had nursed in their arms' (*JB*). Doubt over the detail here does not, of course, diminish in any way the horror of the picture which is being presented.

21. Zion's description of the awful scene continues. **the streets** are littered with bodies, both **young** and **old**. One cause of death is explicitly mentioned by MT and all the Versions (**my maidens and my young men have fallen by the sword**), and LXX connects the verse more firmly to the previous one by adding another (famine: cf. *NEB*). Its text is also different in that it adds (somewhat out of context) a reference to the 'captivity' of the **maidens and young men** (cf. 1:18). What is agreed by all the texts, in line with what the narrator has been saying throughout, is that the carnage is God's responsibility. The **sword** may have belonged to the enemy, but it is really God who has **slain . . . slaughtering without mercy** (cf. vv. 2, 17).

22. Thou didst invite as to the day of an appointed feast my terrors on every side: some doubt surrounds the precise meaning of Heb. *mᵉgûray missābîb*, *RSV*'s **my terrors on every side**. A few modern interpreters (e.g. Ewald, 336–337) have followed the lead of LXX, which derives *mᵉgûray* from the verb *gûr*, 'to sojourn' (cf. *mᵉgûray* in Gen. 47:9), and have translated the phrase: 'my sojourners round about'. The idea in this case would be that people from the towns and villages around Jerusalem fled to the city in the hope of protection, only to be trapped and killed there. Comparison with 1:15, however, where it was claimed that God had 'summoned (Heb. *qārā*') an assembly (Heb. *môʿēd*) against' Zion, suggests that *mᵉgûray* here is a reference to hostile forces rather than Judaeans, and that the imagery of the gathering of people for a religious festival is once more being used to describe the convergence of these forces upon Zion. God has invited (Heb. *qārā*') *mᵉgûray missābîb* **as to the day of an appointed feast** (Heb. *kᵉyôm môʿēd*). The use of *māgôr missābîb* in Jeremiah (6:25; 20:3, 10; 46:5; 49:29; cf. also Ps. 31:13 [MT 31:14]) supports this view, since the *māgôr* of that phrase certainly cannot be related to the verb 'to sojourn'. It could mean 'terror' (deriving it from the verb *gûr*, 'to fear': cf. Isa. 31:9); 'destruction' (from *māgar*, 'to throw, throw down': cf. A. M. Honeyman, 'Magor mis-sabib and Jeremiah's Pun', VT 4 (1954) 424–26); or perhaps 'strife, hostility' (from *gûr*, 'to stir up strife, quarrel'). *mᵉgûray* in our verse is perhaps being used of the sources of these things, possibly natural (e.g. famine) but more probably (in view of the remainder of the verse) human: 'those who terrorize me/bring destruction upon me/are hostile to me', i.e. enemies. These enemies, the agents of God himself, have duly wrought destruction, to the extent, says Zion, that **none escaped or survived**. This is clearly a further example of the hyperbole noted in chapter 1 (cf. the comments, for example, on 1:3, 4), designed to emphasize the magnitude of the catastrophe. It is not strictly consistent with other parts of the poem (e.g. vv. 10, 12).

those whom I dandled and reared my enemy destroyed: the shocking fate of the children of Jerusalem has already been described in v. 20. Here the fate of the inhabitants of the city in general, regarded as mother Zion's children, is referred to. LXX's alternative here, 'I have strengthened and multiplied all my enemies', makes little sense and is probably to be explained as arising from a misunderstanding of MT (Albrektson, *Studies*, 125–126). The immediate cause of the misunderstanding may well have been the rare verb *ṭippaḥ*, *RSV*'s **dandled**, which otherwise occurs only in Isa. 48:13. Its apparent meaning there ('to spread out, to measure out') is clearly not appropriate here. We must therefore guess its meaning from the context, with such help as can be gained from related Heb. words and the cognate languages. The fact that it occurs with Heb. *ribbāh*, 'to rear', suggests either that it is similar in meaning to this (cf. Vulg.'s 'those whom I brought up'; Driver, 'Hebrew Notes', 138–139, 'whom I have nurtured'), or that it refers to the stages strictly prior to the rearing of children, and therefore has something to do with babies or infants. A connection with the nouns *ṭepaḥ* and *ṭōpaḥ*, 'hand-breadth' mentioned above seems possible (cf. BDB, 381), thus 'carried in the hands' (cf. Syr.), and so **dandled** or 'nursed' (*JB*). Alternatively, we might explain the word, in the light of an analogous Arabic expression, as referring to the safe birth of a child rather than its care in the early years (cf. Albrektson, *Studies*, 120): thus *NEB*'s 'brought safely to birth'. Zion's children, cherished from birth, have been brutally murdered.

MAN OF HOPE, MAN OF DESPAIR 3:1–66

There has been some debate among scholars as to the number of the speakers in this third poem, but there seems little solid evidence to suggest that there are any more than two. The first is introduced to us in v. 1 as 'the man' (Heb. *geber*, a word which recurs throughout the initial part of the poem, cf. vv. 27, 35, 39). Some scholars (e.g. Albrektson, *Studies*, 126–128; and most recently, H. Gottlieb, 'Das kultische Leiden des Königs: Zu den Klageliedern 3, 1', *SJOT* 2 (1987) 121–126), taking their cue from a very ancient tradition, have argued that this 'man' is not an individual, but rather Zion and her people as a collective. Both the context and the content of chapter 3, however, render this interpretation implausible. On the one hand, Zion in chapters 1 and 2 is female. The reader who comes to 3:1 via chapter 2 would not naturally assume that the *geber* here is to be identified with her. Nor is this likely, upon further consideration, to have been in the mind of the author; for the third poem was never intended to be read independently of the second, but was rather composed with the second in mind. The reference simply to '*his* wrath' in 3:1, with no further definition of the subject, clearly indicates that 2:22 (with its explicit reference to 'the anger of *the Lord*') and chapter 2 as a whole (with its general theme of 'swallowed up in anger') were always read before it (cf., for example, Budde, 93; Rudolph, 235). On the other hand, 3:48, 51 clearly make a distinction between the one weeping and the people/city, the statement of 3:48 being very similar to that of the narrator in 2:11b. It seems much more likely, then, that it is this narrator, whose voice has already dominated chapters 1 and 2, who himself is the speaker for most of chapter 3. It cannot be denied, of course, that, as in chapters 1 and 2, he feels himself to be closely identified with Zion and her people. Some of the expressions he uses are indeed reminiscent of those used in the earlier poems by Zion (compare, for example, 3:48a with 1:16a). Their suffering is his suffering, and he can exhort them to join him in repentance (cf. vv. 40–42). This is as far as any 'collectivism' goes, however. The narrator may to some extent speak for others, but he certainly speaks, as he has in the other poems, with his own distinct voice. That is not to say that Zion does not speak at all in the third poem. It seems likely that 3:34–36 constitute an objection, spoken by a second voice, to the narrator's message of hope in the preceding verses (see the comment below), vv. 37–39 representing the narrator's response to this objection. The identity of the objector is not revealed. Since in the first and second poems the second speaker is Zion, however, and we have already noted there divergences of opinion between her and the narrator, the natural assumption must be that it is she who speaks here also.

A second point debated among scholars concerned with the interpretation of Lamentations 3 has been to what extent one, to what extent two, situations of suffering are described here. This debate has centred upon the tenses of the verbs in vv. 52–66. Most commentators have believed that the perfect verbs of at least vv. 52–58, if not more, of this passage indicate that it is an experience of suffering and deliverance from the past which is related here. God has already rescued the sufferer speaking here from his former plight, and an account of his experience is included at this point so that the people may have hope in the midst of their present troubles. One difficulty with this view, however, is that it requires us to take v. 56b with its imperative (most unusually) as the content of a past plea to God (so *RSV*'s 'thou didst hear my plea, ''Do not close thine ear to my cry for help!'' ': see the comment on v. 56 below). Another is that it necessitates, given that vv. 63–66 clearly presuppose a present situation of distress (see the comments on vv. 64–66), that we draw a distinction in the passage between two situations of suffering. This cannot plausibly be done, since no convincing point of transition between the two supposed situations can be found.

It is not a very natural reading of the text, for example, to divide it at vv. 58–59 (so Zenner, *Beiträge*, 27; Wiesmann, 197–198), differentiating between 'Thou hast taken up my cause . . .' (the end of the description of past distress) and 'Thou hast seen the wrong done to me . . .' (the beginning of the description of present distress). V. 50 clearly implies that the author of Lamentations 3 believed that being 'seen' by God and being delivered by him go hand in hand. The point at which God takes notice is the point at which lament may cease. It is hardly likely, then, that the author would now imply that God had 'seen' (vv. 59–60) but not yet acted; and v. 63, indeed ('Behold their sitting . . .), suggests that he did not believe that God had yet, in fact, 'seen' his plight. Nor is the suggestion that the transition lies somewhere in vv. 60–63 (Kraus, 54–56; Weiser, 76–77; Kaiser, 349–350, 357–59; cf. *NEB*) any more convincing. The correction of the imperative in v. 59 to a perfect which is necessary if this view is to be plausible *is* supported by LXX, Syr. (see the comment on v. 59); but it is stretching credibility to suppose that the oppression of v. 63 is different from that of some or all of the remainder of the verses. There is absolutely no hint in vv. 60–63 that all the third person masculine plural suffixes ('*their* vengeance', '*their* taunts', '*their* songs' etc.) do not refer to the same people and the same situation.

It is much better, then, to take all of vv. 52–66 as referring to one situation of distress, experienced by the speakers in the poem in the present. The view taken in this commentary is that only the perfect verbs of vv. 52–54 in fact refer to the past. They describe past events with present consequences in terms of suffering. The perfect verbs of vv. 55–61 are to be understood rather differently, v. 55 describing the present and vv. 56–61 expressing, like the imperatives of vv. 56b, 59b (but see the comment below) and 63a, and the imperfects of vv. 64–66, hope for the future. The perfects of vv. 56–61, are therefore, as some commentators have argued (e.g. Gordis, 186–87; Hillers, 15, 52–53, 59; Gottlieb, *Study*, 57–60), 'precative'. They are best rendered in English by the imperative.

The poem opens, then, with a lament by the narrator (vv. 1–18) in which he describes his own experience of the suffering which has come upon his people. God has so afflicted him that he has been reduced to despair: he has lost all hope (v. 18). Vv. 19–21 represent the man in transition between this despair and a renewal of hope, vv. 22–33 going on to express his confidence in ultimate deliverance. One should not complain when confronted by calamity. One should rather wait quietly for God to display his mercy. But what if God is not really in control of events (vv. 34–36)? Is not the faith of the narrator then misplaced? This objection is met in vv. 37–39 with a reassertion of God's sovereignty. He indeed is in control of all happenings, both good and bad. The narrator is therefore right to counsel patience and silence in the face of adversity (v. 39). Having thus argued himself from despair to hope, he is now in a position to offer exhortation and encouragement to others. He summons his fellow-sufferers to repentance and prayer (vv. 40–47), breaking off in grief in v. 48 for yet more lament, though now concerned more with the suffering of others than with his own (vv. 48–51). In vv. 52–66, however, he returns once again to explore his own individual situation, pleading with God for deliverance from his plight. Here the stress is entirely upon suffering as something inflicted and endured by human beings. The categories of sin and judgment by means of which the situation was explained in the early part of the poem are nowhere in evidence. Nor, indeed, are the hopeful utterances there repeated here. We are entitled to see in vv. 52–66, then, a retreat from the confident position adopted in the middle of the poem. Faith and reason have for the moment been overwhelmed by experience.

Lamentations 3, then, reveals that the narrator of chaps 1 and 2 is not quite so sure of himself as his utterances thus far in the book might have led us to believe. He, too, when faced with the reality of suffering, struggles to explain what is happening in terms of his faith, to find hope in the midst of despair. Like most sufferers, he swings from one extreme to the other. He complains, he is driven to doubt. He immediately expresses hope and affirms that silence and patience are good, exhorting himself and others to prayer; and then falls back within himself, complaining and hoping for revenge on his enemies. The central poem of the book does not, then, give us news of the triumph of faith over doubt, as has often been claimed by commentators. It gives us only an interim report on a battle in progress.

For a discussion of the historical circumstances in which this third lament might have been composed, see 'Author, Date and Place of Composition' in the Introduction.

*

1–3. We begin, in the first three verses, with what appears to be a generalised statement of the man's desperate situation. **I am the man who has seen affliction under the rod of his wrath:** elsewhere in the *OT* (e.g. Lam. 1:9), the phrase 'to see affliction' (Heb. *rā'āh 'onî*) is used only of God taking notice of the plight of others. Its use here is thus unusual in two respects. It is a *human being* who is the subject of the verb *rā'āh*; and this verb is being used of 'experiencing, knowing' (cf. *JB, NEB*) rather than of 'seeing' in a physical sense. It is possible that the choice of phrase is intended to emphasize the direness of the narrator's situation. He has received from God, not sympathy, but only the chastisement (with a **rod** or staff) which a slave might receive at the hands of his master (Exod. 21:20). It is certainly the case, as Hillers, 66, points out, that a similar contrast is intended in the second verse.

Divine leading in the *OT*, like the shepherd's leading of his sheep (cf. Heb. *nāhag*, **he has driven**, of driving flocks in Exod. 3:1 and other places), is usually for the benefit of the party being led (e.g. Isa. 63:11–14). It is a leading into **light**, symbolic of all that is good. God has **brought** this man, however, **into darkness** (cf. Amos 5:18), the abode of the dead (cf. v. 6). His **hand** is truly against him.

4–6. In these verses and those which follow (7–18), the narrator describes his suffering at greater length, using metaphors and turns of phrase well known from lament psalms and other *OT* writings such as Job. The stereotypical nature of the language, indeed, together with the generous use of hyperbole, make it very difficult to gain any impression of the concrete nature of the suffering. It is tempting to take the first part of v. 4 (**He has made my flesh and my skin waste away**), for example, as an allusion to emaciation brought about by hunger. Allusions to hunger are found in all the other poems of Lamentations, and the two other references to effects on the **skin** in the book are both made in the context of descriptions of famine (4:7–10, 5:9–10). The use of the siege metaphor in v. 5 fits particularly well with such an idea. The narrator as an individual, like the people as a whole, has endured the famine brought about by siege and conquest. We simply cannot be sure that this interpretation is correct, however, since it is not clear whether the statement is meant literally or not. It certainly seems likely that the second part of v. 4 (**and broken my bones**), like other parts of the poem, is *not* meant literally; and suffering is described elsewhere in the *OT* in terms similar to those found here, yet without hunger apparently being in mind (cf. Mic. 3:1–3; Ps. 38:3 [MT 38:4]).

he has besieged and enveloped me with bitterness and tribulation: *JB*'s very different 'he has made a yoke for me, has encircled my head with weariness' rests partly upon repointing, partly upon emendation, and partly upon following LXX in taking Heb. *rō'š* as 'head' rather than as the bitter and poisonous herb of Ps. 69:21 [MT 69:22] and other texts, sometimes known as 'gall' (cf. v. 19 below). The Heb. text as we have it, however, makes perfect sense.

like the dead of long ago: or better, 'like those long dead' (*NIV*,
cf. also *NEB*). Sheol, the *OT* abode of the dead, is often characterized
as a place of darkness (e.g. Ps. 88:12 [MT 88:13]; Job 10:20–22),
the residents of which are cut off from and forgotten by God. The
narrator's situation, he feels, is analogous to theirs. Dwelling **in
darkness** is also the lot of the prisoner, of course (cf. Ps. 107:10–16;
Isa. 42:6–7), and v. 6 therefore leads neatly into v. 7.

7–9. The lament continues, the metaphors for distress in these
verses being imprisonment and obstruction. God has **walled** (Heb.
gādar) the man in and placed him in **chains** (lit. 'bronze', which
on several occasions in the *OT*, but only here in the singular, is
shorthand for 'bronze fetters') whose weight inhibits movement.
Furthermore, he is impervious to the cries of the victim. Not only
does he shut the narrator in, he **shuts out** his **prayer**. He has
blocked (Heb. *gādar*) his **ways with hewn stones** (Syr. 'thorns';
LXX has no equivalent, probably due to corruption in the Greek
text, cf. Albrektson, *Studies*, 132–133). He **has made** his **paths
crooked**, because the narrator is forced to deviate from his chosen
route, picking his way past the obstructions. God has disrupted
his journey along the path of life, frustrating his purposes.

10–12. Further perils along the path are described, although
the detail of what the author has in mind is not clear. V. 10 is
straightforward enough: God has lain in wait for him **like a bear
. . . like a lion**, ready to pounce. It is with v. 11 that the problems
occur. The Heb. of the first part of the verse is *dᵉrākay sôrēr
wayᵉpaśśᵉḥēnî*, which *RSV* renders **he led me off my way and tore
me to pieces**. *sôrēr* in this case is regarded (with Syr., Vulg.) as
a form of the verb *sûr*, 'to turn aside' (cf. Brandscheidt, *Gotteszorn
und Menschenleid*, 21); *wayᵉpaśśᵉḥēnî* (also with Syr. and Vulg.) as
deriving from a verb *piśśaḥ*, 'to tear in pieces', which occurs only
here in the *OT*; and the verse as a whole as a continuation of the
metaphors in vv. 9 and 10. God is pictured at one and the same
time as the one who has forced the traveller off the path by placing
obstacles in his way, and as the wild beasts who attack him when
he leaves it. *NIV* interprets *sôrēr* and *wayᵉpaśśᵉḥēnî* similarly, but
connects v. 11 only with v. 10: 'he dragged me from the path and

mangled me'. *JB*, in contrast, adopts a mediaeval interpretation of *sôrēr* (accepted by Rudolph, 230, among others), deriving it from the noun *sîr*, 'thorn' ('he has filled my paths with briars and torn me'). *NEB* thinks (with LXX) that the verb is *sārar*, 'to be stubborn, rebellious' (cf. *sôrēr* in Dt. 21:18 and many other places in the *OT*), connecting *wayᵉpašᵉʿḥēnî* (with Aq.) with *pāsaḥ*, 'to limp, be lame': 'he has made my way refractory and lamed me'. LXX translates *wayᵉpašᵉʿḥēnî* as 'he has brought me to an end, to a standstill', which some commentators (e.g. Albrektson, *Studies*, 135–136) have thought might be correct. It is simply impossible to be certain about the meaning of this part of the verse. Its second part, Heb. *śāmanî šōmēm*, can also be rendered in a number of ways (cf. the comments on the root *šmm* at 1:4). It could mean that God has left the man **desolate** (cf. also *NEB*), which *NIV* interprets as meaning 'without help', but which could also mean 'wretched, in despair'. Alternatively, it might mean that he has made him an object of horror among those who know or observe him (*JB*).

he bent his bow and set me as a mark for his arrow: with v. 12 we are on more secure ground. The imagery has changed: in this and the next verse, God is portrayed as an archer who has the narrator in his sights as a target (cf. 2:4).

13–15. He drove into my heart the arrows of his quiver: lit. 'he drove into my kidneys . . .'. Like other major organs (cf. the comments on 2:11–12), the kidneys are sometimes regarded as a seat of the emotions (e.g. Job 19:27; Prov. 23:16). *RSV*'s translation is therefore justified (God has thrown the man into great distress), although the idea that serious damage had been done to him would also be communicated by a more literal translation (*JB, NEB*).

I have become the laughingstock of all peoples: *RSV* (with *NEB*) follows the Sebir (an ancient Jewish textual note, of disputed significance: cf. Gordis, 177), many of the ancient Heb. mss. and Syr. in reading Heb. *ʿammîm*, **peoples**, interpreting those laughing (as in 1:7, where the root *śḥq* also appears) as foreigners. This reading is certainly preferable in terms of sense to that of the majority of Heb. mss. (cf. LXX, Vulg.; *AV, JB* and *NIV*), which have *ʿammî*, 'my people', implying that the mockers are Israelites.

This simply does not fit with the tone of other sections of the poem, in which the speaker identifies himself with his people (cf. vv. 40-48), but seeks vengeance on his persecutors (cf. vv. 61-66, particularly v. 63, where he repeats that he is the subject of **their songs**). The verse should rather be interpreted as yet another example of the narrator individualizing and making personal the fate of the whole people. He, in common with them, has had to endure the taunts of those who observe their suffering (cf. particularly vv. 45-46), making them the subject **of their songs all day long**.

He has filled me with bitterness, he has sated me with wormwood: a plant with a strong, bitter taste, **wormwood** appears in the *OT* as a symbol of bitterness, sorrow or calamity (cf. also Am. 5:7, 6:12; Prov. 5:4). The allusion here appears to be to a drink made from this plant, since Heb. *rwh*, **sated**, in other contexts refers to saturation by liquid (e.g. Isa. 55:10).

16-18. He has made my teeth grind on gravel, and made me cower in ashes: the second verb of this verse is found only here in the *OT*, while the first occurs otherwise only in Ps. 119:20, where its precise meaning is not clear. The picture being presented here is consequently also not clear. Is it the consumption of **gravel** which is in view, the imagery of the consumption of unpleasant things being continued from v. 15 (cf. Prov. 20:17 and the ancient rabbinic interpretation of the phrase)? Or is the reference to abasement, as in the colloquial English expression 'to rub someone's face in the dirt' (cf. the analogous 'May . . . his enemies lick the dust' in Ps. 72:9 and a similar reference to self-abasement in v. 29 of the present chapter)? If the latter is correct, then we might have a parallel to it in the second part of the line, with its reference to **ashes**. *RSV* (cf. also Syr.) clearly thinks that this is also a reference to the narrator's lowly state, as does *NIV*: 'he has trampled me in the dust'. It is possible, on the other hand, that in the latter part of the verse there is still a further continuation of the imagery of v. 15. LXX continues the metaphor of consumption ('he fed me ashes': cf. *JB, NEB*), while some commentators (e.g. Kraus, 61) have argued that the reference is to failure to provide a place to sleep. Throughout vv. 15–16, they maintain, God is pictured as a host who turns all the conventions of hospitality on their head.

my soul is bereft of peace: *RSV*, in common with most modern translations, apparently follows Syr. and Vulg. in reading the verb in this phrase as a third person feminine passive: lit. 'my soul is rejected from peace'. In MT, it is either a third person feminine active (though this is unlikely) or a second person masculine active, God being the subject: 'you have rejected my soul from peace' (cf. *AV*). LXX goes its own way in having a third person masculine active: 'he has rejected my soul from peace' (favoured by Kaiser, 343). These variations make little difference to the sense. It is worth noting, however, that whereas many of the translations of the Heb., including most of the modern English ones, paraphrase it so as to make the line say that it is 'peace' which has moved or departed, the picture in the Heb. itself is of the movement of the narrator. It is not so much that peace has left him, more that he has been banished from the realm of peace (cf. Kraus, 61). *JB*'s 'my soul is shut out from peace' is therefore perhaps the best of the modern renderings. His suffering is such that the memory of his pleasant life before it began has all but been obliterated. He has **forgotten what happiness** (or 'prosperity' with *AV, NEB* and *NIV*) **is**.

Gone is my glory, and my expectation from the LORD: exactly how we should understand Heb. *niṣî*, **glory**, is not clear. *RSV* and *NIV* ('splendour'), following LXX and Syr., apparently take it to refer to the narrator's previously prosperous and happy state, mentioned in v. 17, though this would be the only occasion in the *OT* upon which *nēṣaḥ* is an attribute of a human being rather than of God (cf. I Sam. 15:29; I Chr. 29:11). It would be possible also, of course, to interpret their translation as itself referring to God. Kraus, 61, argues that the phrase refers to the disappearance of God from the narrator's life. It does not seem probable, however, that the verb *'ābad*, 'to perish' (*RSV*'s **Gone**), would be used in such a context. It seems more likely that we should translate *niṣî* here as 'my strength, endurance' (*AV, JB* and *NEB*; Dahood, 'Readings', 184–185, though taking the word to be from a different root), rendering the line either as 'My strength has gone, and my hope in the LORD', or, as Hillers, 50, suggests, 'My lasting hope in Yahweh has perished'.

This is perhaps the lowest point of the whole poem. The catalogue of suffering which the narrator has endured has so taken its toll that even the hope which might make it tolerable seems to have deserted him. He is a man in the deepest despair. Yet as Hillers, 69, points out, we are also at a point of transition in the poem. As with other instances in *OT* laments in which statements prefaced by **I say** or 'I said, thought' appear (e.g. Ps. 31:22 [MT 31:23]), we are about to hear another, more positive side to the story. What we see here, in fact, is a man in dialogue with himself. His experience, recounted thus far, pushes him towards despair. His faith as presented in the verses to be discussed below, however, tells him that hope is not futile. The juxtaposition of the seemingly contradictory vv. 18 and 21 captures well the inner tensions of all people of faith who also face the realities of human existence squarely and without pretence.

19-21. A difficult stanza, from the point of view of both text and interpretation. The problems of the former will be clear enough from the following discussion, but a summary of the difficulties of the latter might be of some help to the reader at this point. To begin with what is clear: the transition hinted at in v. 18 is clearly carried through in this stanza, the despair of vv. 1–18 giving way to the confidence of vv. 22 ff. What is not clear is the manner in which this transition is achieved. Interpreters have disagreed, in the first place, as to whether v. 19 is part of the general complaint or a plea to God to take notice of the narrator's plight. They have differed, secondly, as to whether v. 20 is either of these things or an expression of confidence in God. And they have had contrary opinions, thirdly, as to whether the grounds for the expression of hope in v. 21 are to be found solely in vv. 22 ff. or are partly present within this stanza itself. A more detailed analysis of these different possibilities follows below.

Remember my affliction and my bitterness, the wormwood and the gall!: MT may either be translated 'remember my affliction and my wandering, the wormwood and the gall' (taking Heb. *zᵉkor* as an imperative); or, with *NEB*, 'the memory of my distress and my wanderings is wormwood and gall' (taking it as an infinitive construct). The ancient Versions in general favour the former interpretation (Syr., Vulg.), though LXX has 'I remembered', which is more in line with the latter. Whether this verse is a plea to God or simply a statement is therefore not clear, and the context does not help us to decide. *RSV*'s **bitterness** assumes, as the same rendering does in 1:7, that MT is corrupt, the Heb. letter r (*mᵉrôrî*) having become confused with the similar-looking d (*mᵉrûdî*). As in 1:7, however, there is no Versional support for such an emendation. It is, indeed, difficult to believe that an original *mᵉrôrî* could have become corrupt at this point in the poem, with vv. 5 and 15 so closely preceding, and the following reference to **wormwood** and **gall** making the reference so natural. The mention of 'wandering' is quite appropriate, on the other hand, since the narrator is describing what has happened to him as one of Zion's people, and 1:7 (as well as other verses) tells us that this people had to endure exile.

My soul continually thinks of it and is bowed down within me: the Qere in this verse has the second finite verb as *wᵉtāšôaḥ*, from a root *šwḥ* or *šḥḥ*, 'to be bowed down'. Other texts also speak of the **soul** being **bowed down** (Ps. 42:5, 6, 11 [MT 42:6, 7, 12]; 43:5; 44:25 [MT 44:26]), meaning that the person is enduring, to quote Albrektson, *Studies*, 142, n. 4, 'oppression by sorrows or enemies'. The Kethib has the verb either as *wᵉtāšîaḥ*, probably also to be derived from *šwḥ*, or as *wᵉtāśîaḥ*, from *śyḥ*, 'to meditate, talk, complain' (cf. LXX). We might render MT in the latter case as 'my soul continually thinks of it and complains within me' (cf. Job 7:11). This brings us, however, to the major problem of the verse: whether part or all of it is addressed directly to God. The majority opinion has been that Heb. *napšî*, **my soul**, is the subject of the whole sentence. This view is taken, for example, by LXX (or at least, by those Greek mss. which divide vv. 19–20 in the same way as MT: see Albrektson, *Studies*, 141); by Targ. and Vulg.; and by *RSV, JB* and *NIV*. A few interpreters have, however, followed the lead of Syr. in taking the first finite verb of the line as a second person masculine rather than a third person feminine, some giving this imperatival force (cf. *NEB*'s 'Remember, O remember') and others taking it as an expression of confidence (e.g. Albrektson, *Studies*, 141–145: 'Yea, thou wilt surely remember'). Some of these interpreters, indeed, have thought that *both* verbs have God as their subject, emending MT's *napšî* to *napšekā*, 'your soul' (Gottwald, *Studies*, 13; Albrektson, *Studies*, 141–143; cf. *NEB*'s '. . . stoop down [lit. 'let your soul stoop down'] to me'), on the assumption that we have here one of the famous Tiqqune Hassopherim. These were early scribal corrections to statements which contained elements, like the attribution in this example of a 'soul' to God, which were thought to detract from God's dignity. There is no clear evidence, however, that *napšekā* ever was a reading found in a Heb. text, nor does this reading in any case make such good sense in the context (cf. Hillers, 55–56; Gordis, 178–179). Either of the other two interpretations of the line seem possible, though much depends upon the view of v. 19 which is adopted. It seems likely that the sense of vv. 19–20 together is either 'Remember (Heb. *zkr*) . . . for I (lit. 'my soul') *certainly* remember (*zkr*)'; 'Remember . . . you will surely remember; or 'I remember . . . I well remember'. *NEB*'s interpretation of vv. 19–20 as a statement *followed* by a plea to God lacks the power and coherence of any of these alternatives.

But this I call to mind, and therefore I have hope: there is no Heb. equivalent to *RSV*'s **But**, which is present because the way in which *RSV* has interpreted vv. 19–20 requires that v. 21 be understood as the beginning of a new section. Vv. 19–20 represent the end of a complaint, in which no grounds for hope exist (cf. v. 18), and the **this** of v. 21, which provides the ground for hope, must therefore refer to what follows in vv. 22 ff. This is, indeed, the generally accepted interpretation of v. 21 (cf. *JB*, *NEB*, *NIV*). If the beginning of v. 20 is understood with some commentators (e.g. Albrektson, *Studies*, 141–145) as an expression of confidence in God, of course, the **But** would not be necessary. Albrektson renders vv. 20–21 thus: 'Yea, thou wilt surely remember, and thy soul will give heed to me. This I call to mind, therefore I have hope'. In this case vv. 22 ff. are simply a continuation of the expression of hope found in v. 20–21.

22–24. After the uncertainties of the previous stanza, we are now on firmer ground. The tone of the poem has clearly changed from one of despair to one of hope and confidence. It is interesting to note that vv. 22–24 are not present in the LXX. This is presumably because the similarity between the conclusions of this and the previous stanza (vv. 21b and 24b) has led a translator or copyist to overlook the intervening material, a phenomenon known to textual critics as 'homoioteleuton'.

The steadfast love of the LORD never ceases, his mercies never come to an end: *RSV* follows one Heb. ms., Syr. and Targ. in reading the first verb as a third person plural which has **steadfast love** as its subject (cf. also *JB* and *NIV*). MT, on the other hand, has a first person plural (cf. also Aq., Symm., some other Greek mss., OL and Vulg.), 'we have not come to an end, been consumed'. The problem then is how to understand the whole line. *NEB* pronounces the Heb. 'unintelligible', which it clearly is not. We could render it either as 'It is because of the steadfast love of the LORD that we are not consumed, that his mercies never come to an end' (similarly Albrektson, *Studies*, 145–146), or as 'Because of the LORD's great love we are not consumed, for his compassions never fail' (*NIV*, cf. *AV*). Perhaps even better than these, if the assumption is that v. 21 refers forwards rather than backwards, would be the following translation of vv. 21–23a: 'But this I call to mind, and therefore have hope: the steadfast love of the LORD! For we are not consumed because his mercies never come to an end: they are new every morning'. This understanding of the double *kî* of v. 22 gains support in particular from the book of Job (e.g. 8:9, 24:17), parallels with which are everywhere to be found in Lamentations 3. However one reads the verb, of course, what is quite clear is that the narrator is grounding his hope in God's **love** or 'covenant loyalty' (Heb. *ḥesed*). It is this which leads God to act in a consistently merciful way. MT's text simply makes it particularly clear that the expression of hope begins from the realisation that the people of whom the narrator is a member, however desperate their situation might be, have at least survived. They have 'not been consumed', and this in itself is a sign that

God is gracious. The covenant between God and his people is still intact, and therefore hope remains that things will improve.

great is thy faithfulness: *JB* and *NEB* unnecessarily emend the second person suffix to a third person suffix, 'his faithfulness'. We have noted sudden changes in address before in the poems of Lamentations. Heb. style seems to find no difficulty with these.

The LORD is my portion: Heb. *ḥeleq* is a piece or a portion of something, most often used in the *OT* of a tract of land (e.g. Jos. 19:9). Israel is described as God's piece of land or dwelling place in Dt. 32:9, and God as the 'dwelling place' of Israelites in Num. 18:20; Jer. 10:16, 51:19; and several of the Psalms (e.g. 16:5, 142:5 [MT 142:6]). What such language probably signifies is best seen from Num. 18:20, with its distinction between the earthly territories of the people in general and the spiritual 'territory' (God himself) of the priests. The people were to be sustained in the normal way by the produce of their land, while the priests owed their survival directly to God himself, who provided for them from the offerings which he received (cf. Num. 18:8 ff.). When the narrator affirms that God is his **portion**, then, he is both affirming where his commitment ultimately lies (in the spiritual rather than the merely physical realm: this is where he 'lives') and recognizing something fundamental about his relationship with God (that he is entirely dependent upon God for his survival). To someone who has faced such calamity in the earthly realm, and has apparently lost his physical territory (cf. the comments on v. 19), the belief that God represents his 'real' dwelling place is naturally comforting, and a source of hope: **therefore I will hope in him**.

25-27. Each of the lines of this stanza begins, not only with the same letter, but with the same word (Heb. *ṭôb*, 'good'). The first line affirms that God is **good** to those who in a situation of distress engage in patient prayer. In the second and third lines it is not quite clear whether it is likewise being claimed that God is good to people, or whether it is the response of the sufferer and the suffering itself which are thought to be good. The Heb. allows either interpretation.

It is good that one should wait quietly for the salvation of

the **LORD:** the first part of MT (*ṭôb wᵉyāḥîl wᵉdûmām*) is difficult here. The intent seems to be that we should read *yāḥîl* as an imperfect from the rare verbal root *ḥwl* or *ḥyl* (cf. Ps. 10:5, Job 20:21), 'to be firm, strong', and *dûmām* as the rare noun 'silence' found in Isa. 47:5 and Hab. 2:19, though used adverbially as in the Isaiah text. An attempt at rendering MT could be made along the following lines: 'It is good that one should endure without complaint, (waiting) for the salvation of the LORD'. This gives much the same sense as *RSV* and the other modern translations, even though they all diverge slightly from MT. The ancient Versions also for the most part contain the same idea, the exception being Syr., which equally plausibly interprets the **good** as referring to God. We might translate in this case: 'Good is he, when one endures without complaint . . .' (cf. also Wiesmann, 183; Gottlieb, *Study*, 47). What is clear in any case is that appropriate behaviour when faced with calamity includes suffering in silence. Presumably the narrator realises that he himself has not displayed such resoluteness in vv. 1–18! After an onslaught of doubt, he is persuading himself to adopt once more what he regards as a posture of faith.

It is good for a man that he bear the yoke in his youth: or 'He is good towards a man when he bears a yoke in his youth' (Gottlieb, *Study*, 47). The use of Heb. *geber*, man, here emphasizes the change of attitude in these verses which was noted a moment ago. The poem opens with a complaint beginning 'I am the man (*geber*)'. Now the speaker is lauding the virtue of **a man** bearing **the yoke** in silence! The context, and particularly vv. 28–30, makes it more than probable that **the yoke** which is referred to is the yoke of suffering, rather than the yoke of the commandments (Targ.). *RSV*'s interpretation implies more clearly than Gottlieb's that suffering, though a burden like **the yoke** which oxen must carry, is of some benefit to the sufferer. Though it is not specified what that benefit might be, the thought is probably that suffering has an educational and disciplinary, even a redemptive value. As **the yoke** serves to keep the oxen on a straight course, so suffering is God's means of keeping his people on a straight course throughout the journey of life. The beginning of this journey is especially important, as several Heb. proverbs recognize (e.g. Prov. 13:24, 23:13–14). The notion that discipline is essential if the young are to make a good start was firmly entrenched in Israelite society, as it has been in other societies since. The reading **in his youth** is probably to be preferred, then, to the 'from his youth' of some Heb. and Gk. mss. and Vulg. (cf. *JB*), which implies that the narrator has suffered all his life.

28–30. The theme of 'correct behaviour when confronted by calamity', what one should do when the yoke of suffering is **laid** upon one by God, is continued in this stanza. McDaniel, 'Studies', 38–42, argues that the first part of v. 28 (Heb. *yēšēb bādād wᵉyiddōm*) refers to moaning and mourning, rather than **silence** and isolation. There is, however, little justification for this interpretion. There is no certain parallel anywhere for *bdd*, 'to moan' (cf. Gottlieb, *Study*, 48–49), while *yāšᵉbāh bādād* in 1:1, as McDaniel himself acknowledges, is best translated 'she sits alone' (see comment on 1:1). The root *dmm*, by contrast, does appear to have the meaning 'to wail, mourn', in at least one other place in the *OT* (Isa. 23:2). As in 2:10 (see comment), however, the context suggests that its usually accepted meaning, 'to be silent', is better here. Not only is there the reference to **silence** in the previous stanza, but v. 29 can be taken as indicating what the sufferer should do with **his mouth** instead of using it for speech: he should **put** it **in the dust**, an act of self-abasement, in the **hope** that things may yet improve. **Let him sit alone in silence** should be retained, then. What is not clear is whether the isolation is self-imposed in this instance or, as in 1:1, a result of the sufferer being abandoned. In the third line, **let him give his cheek to the smiter, and be filled with insults** (or 'endure full measure of abuse', *NEB*), **the smiter** may either refer to God or, more probably, to fellow human beings (cf. v. 61). In the latter case the point is that one should not *even* respond to those fellow human beings who rain down upon one physical and verbal abuse. Complete passivity is what is required in the face of suffering.

31–33. The character of God is further described as the ground for hope in the midst of dire circumstances. He is not vindictive. His nature is to **have compassion** and to show **steadfast love** towards mankind, and such affliction as he imposes is not imposed **willingly** (lit. 'from his heart'). The implication is that he is compelled by circumstances to do so, specifically by the sins of the sufferer (cf. v. 39). This is good news, for it is possible then to envisage that the period of affliction might come to an end: **he will not cast off for ever**.

34-36. This is a difficult stanza. The natural assumption would be that the same voice is speaking here as in vv. 1–33. In this case, the latter part of v. 36 (Heb. *ʾdōnâ lōʾ rāʾāh*) is best taken either as a statement, **the Lord does not approve** (i.e. look with pleasure upon, cf. also *NEB*: LXX's 'has not commanded' is implausible in the context); or as a question, 'does not the Lord see . . .?' (and, by implication, care about: *JB*, cf. Targ., *NIV*). In both cases the claim is similar to that in vv. 31–33. Although God is indeed responsible for bringing down the judgment which has fallen upon the narrator and his fellow-countrymen (here described in terms of the maltreatment of **prisoners** and the perversion of justice, presumably, in this context, by their conquerors), his heart is not really in it. Judgement is not something which God finds it easy to dispense. It is difficult on this interpretation to see, however, how vv. 37–38 follow on from vv. 34–36. For vv. 37–38 seem to be the response to an *objection* to the narrator's speech. He has maintained throughout that God is responsible for what has happened, and vv. 37–38 apparently reaffirm this in the face of an assertion to the contrary. They do not, therefore, follow on entirely happily from vv. 34–36 as interpreted above. It is possible, of course, that the author has simply anticipated such an objection, and has not felt it necessary to express it in the text. It seems better, however, to understand vv. 34–36 themselves, as Rudolph, 240–241, has suggested, as constituting the objection implied by vv. 37–38. In this case we should translate *ʾdōnâ lōʾ rāʾāh* as a statement, 'the Lord does not see'. Rudolph understands this as a denial that God is *concerned* about the matters under discussion, which does not seem to lead in to the following verses any more felicitously than the possibilities mentioned above. We should rather take it as a denial of sovereignty. Events are taking place of which God has no knowledge (Vulg., cf. *rāʾāh* in 3:1) and over which he has no control. The implication is, of course, that the faith which the narrator has expressed is misplaced. If God is not ultimately responsible for evil, what hope can there be for its removal? It is true that the separation of vv. 31–33 and vv. 34–36 in this way does make the word order as it is found in the latter verses rather unusual (Hillers, 57–58), the three infinitives preceding the finite verb upon which they depend. This feature of the stanza is, however, adequately explained by the need of the author, because of the acrostic nature of the poem, to begin each verse with the letter *l*.

Another interesting feature of vv. 34–36 is the awkwardness of language which results, whichever understanding of these verses is adopted, from the attempt to express the idea that God is transcendent, apart from the world of men, and yet intimately involved in their thoughts and actions and ultimately responsible for them. The author is, of course, not the only theological writer in history to find difficulty in expressing such an idea. God is both the one who 'crushes under his feet' (the English translations tend to obscure the suffix, which makes it clear that the feet belong to God) **all the prisoners** and the one who denies a man justice **in the presence of the Most High**! However we translate *ʾdōnâ lōʾ rāʾāh* in v. 36, then, we have the paradoxical picture of God standing apart from events for which he is described as responsible elsewhere in the stanza.

37–39. Some scholars (e.g. Gordis, 181–83; Dahood, 'Readings', 187) have argued that vv. 37–38 make assertions rather than asking questions. This cannot be correct, however, since the remainder of the chapter makes clear that God is responsible for what has happened. V. 37b cannot be rendered, then, 'the Lord has not ordained it'. More plausibly, S. Weissblueth, 'It is not from the mouth of the Most High that good and evil comes (Lam. 3:38)', *Beth Mikra* 32 (1986–87) 64–67, argues that v. 38 alone is to be taken as a statement, affirming man's responsibility for his actions in the context of divine sovereignty. This is not the most natural way of taking the line after v. 37, however. Both vv. 37 and 38 are best understood as the narrator reasserting his basic premise. God is indeed the source of all things, both good and bad (it is **from the mouth of the Most High that good and evil come**). Nothing can happen **unless the Lord has ordained it**. The narrator has been right, then, to insist that the suffering which he and his fellows have been enduring comes from God. He has been right, too, to express hope; for what God gives, he can take away.

Why should a living man complain, a man, about the punishment of his sins?: MT has often been adjudged corrupt by commentators, who have objected mainly to the unusual expression ʾādām ḥâ, **living man** (e.g. Rudolph, 232) and to the lack of a verb in the latter part of the line (cf. *JB*, Dahood, 'Readings', 187). It seems perfectly comprehensible as it stands, however, and the Versions, though there is some evidence from Syr. and Targ. that the rare verbal root ʾnn caused some difficulties, all reflect a similar text here. The adjective **living**, first of all, can be understood as emphatic: **why should a living man** (i.e. a man who has held on to life) **complain . . .?** Where there is life there is hope: he is in a far better position than those who have actually perished as a result of the troubles (cf. the comment on 3:22). The verb of the first part of the line, secondly, may quite easily be understood as that of its second part also, as it is in *RSV*'s translation. The real difficulty of the verse is not with either of these things, but with the interpretation of its last two words, Heb. ʿal-ḥăṭāʾâw (the Kethib is the singular ḥeṭʾô). *RSV*'s rendering (cf. also *NIV*) of the second part of the line is perfectly possible (*contra* Gottlieb, *Study*, 52: among other instances in which ḥēṭʾ appears to mean 'punishment for sin' rather than simply 'sin' are Isa. 53:12 and Ezek. 23:49), but so is *NEB*'s ('any mortal who has sinned'). We might also take our cue from Budde, 96, and interpret it as the response to the question rather than part of it: 'What *should* the living man complain about? each about his sins!' Whichever of these is correct, the basic assertion of the line is clear enough: a sinful man should not **complain** about his circumstances. This may be seen as a return to the main theme of vv. 21 ff., after a digression to deal with the objection of vv. 34–36. The speaker, having himself opened the poem with a complaint beginning 'I am the man (Heb. *geber*)', had arrived at the conclusion that the correct response to his plight was rather silence and patience (vv. 25–30): a man (*geber*) should 'bear the yoke in his youth' (v. 27). The objector had suggested, on the other hand, that this was futile, since God had no control over what was happening (cf. *geber* again in v. 35). Having dismissed this view in vv. 37–38, the speaker reasserts his position in v. 39, and thus brings this first section of the poem neatly to a close. The **man** whose complaint was so readily and in so detailed a way expressed in vv. 1–20 has persuaded himself that complaint is not justified. The mention of **sins** explicitly for the first time opens up the way to a more constructive response to his plight and that of his listeners, already hinted at in vv. 25–30: repentant prayer. It is such prayer that we find in the passage which immediately follows.

40–42. The narrator has thus far mainly been concerned with himself. He has reflected on his own suffering, struggled with the doubts which this has engendered, and persuaded himself back to what he regards as a position of faith and hope. He has now reached a point where he feels able to offer exhortation and encouragement to others. He summons his people to self-examination and repentance (**Let us test and examine our ways, and return to the LORD**), leading on to sincere prayer to God: they are to **lift up their hearts and hands to God in heaven**. The lifting up of the **hands** was a common gesture in prayer (cf. Ps. 28:2, 63:4 [MT 63:5]), and the Heb. here (*niśśā᾽ lᵉbābēnû ᵓel-kappāyīm*) implies either that the **hearts** are to be lifted up *upon* their **hands** (so LXX and Syr.: the people are to present their innermost feelings to God in prayer) or that **hearts** are to be lifted up *as well as* **hands** (so Vulg.: they are not to remain content merely with the outward forms of prayer, they are to enter into it wholeheartedly). Though many commentators (e.g. Kraus, 53; Meek, 27; and cf. *JB*'s footnote to v. 42) seem unaware of the fact, Heb. *ᵓel* can have both these meanings (cf. Jg. 6:39 and Lev. 18:18, for example), and there is neither need nor justification here for repointing or emendation of MT such as that, for example, which lies behind *NEB*.

We have transgressed and rebelled, and thou hast not forgiven: with this confession of sin in v. 43 begins the content of the prayer which the speaker wishes his compatriots to join him in uttering. It continues until v. 47, when the plural form gives way once again to the singular.

43-45. Thou hast wrapped thyself with anger and pursued us, slaying without pity: *RSV* (with *JB* and *NIV*: *NEB* unnecessarily and with no Versional support emends the text) understands the Heb. verb *sakkōtāh* here (**Thou hast wrapped**) as reflexive. God clothes himself **with anger**, as an enemy might put on his battle apparel, in order to fight against his people. Certainly *sakkôtāh be'ānān lāk* in v. 44 refers to God clothing himself (**thou hast wrapped thyself with a cloud**), on this occasion with the intention of making himself inaccessible to **prayer**. In that verse, however, there is a pronoun with suffix (*lāk*) which explicitly indicates that the verb is reflexive. *skk* in the Qal by itself, as it is in v. 43, does not otherwise have a reflexive significance in the *OT*. The first part of this line may therefore be better translated: 'thou hast enveloped *us* with anger' (so, for example, Hillers, 59, and Gottlieb, *Study*, 53). Both verses contain reminiscences of earlier themes. The notion of **prayer** being shut out is found in v. 8, while the picture of God as a warrior, **slaying** his people **without pity**, appears earlier at 2:2, 4, 17, 21.

Thou hast made us offscouring and refuse among the peoples: Heb. *s'ḥî* **offscouring**, occurs only here in the *OT*. It is usually thought to be related to the verb *sḥh* which appears in Ezek. 26:4b ('. . . and I will scrape [*w'siḥêtî*] her soil from her, and make her a bare rock'): thus *RSV*'s rendering and *NIV*'s 'scum'. If this is correct, then the thought is that people regard Israel with the same distaste as they would their bodily waste and rubbish, and treat her accordingly. There are several earlier references, of course, to the contemptuous attitude of those observing Israel's difficulties (cf. v. 14; 1:7-8; 2:15-16), and there can be little doubt, in view of v.46, that it is to this that v. 45 also refers. The *precise* meaning of the line cannot in the nature of things be certain, however, particularly since the Versions have no reference to rubbish here. LXX refers to blindness and rejection, Syr. and Vulg. to uprootedness and contempt or rejection (see Albrektson, *Studies*, 157–158).

46–48. All our enemies rail against us: another link with earlier material (cf. 2:16a). **panic and pitfall have come upon us, devastation and destruction:** two pairs of words (*paḥad wāpaḥat* and *haššē't wᵉhaššāber*) beginning with the same consonants and, particularly in the case of the first pair, sounding similar, are chosen by the Hebrew author here to describe the calamity, and *RSV* makes a particularly good attempt at capturing this stylistic flourish in its translation. *paḥad wāpaḥat* is literally 'fear and pit' (cf. also Isa. 24:17 and Jer. 48:43), an allusion to the plight of the hunted animal who must flee the hunter whilst avoiding the traps which he has set (cf. the comment on 1:13). The Versions (with the exception of Vulg.) offer a more general, most often a synonymous, expression alongside 'fear' (LXX having 'anger' or 'astonishment', Syr. and Targ. 'trembling'). They also have a different text in the second part of the verse. LXX and Vulg. (and a few Heb. mss.) understand *s't*, which would be a hapax legomenon as pointed by MT, as from the verb *nāśa'*, 'to lift up' rather than as from the verb *šā'āh*, 'to crash into ruins', while Syr. rather strangely has 'pit' and Targ. another word meaning 'trembling'.

my eyes flow with rivers of tears because of the destruction of the daughter of my people: suddenly we are back in the singular, and the speaker is describing his feelings again, though now about the sufferings of others rather than his own. The reference to **destruction** (Heb. *šeber*) in the previous verse acts as the catalyst for an outpouring of grief about it in this and the following three verses. It is as if the corporate attempt to rehearse the disaster before God has proved too much for him. It has overwhelmed him emotionally, and has led him to break off the prayer of repentance in favour of yet further lament.

49–51. My eyes will flow without ceasing, without respite: there is some disagreement in the textual tradition as to whether the first part of this verse refers to weeping itself (MT, most Gk. mss., Syr.) or to the effects of weeping on the eyes (some Gk. mss. and Vulg.: cf. 2:11), and LXX additionally makes the speaker rather than his eyes the subject of the second verb ('I shall not be silent'). The final phrase of MT (Heb. *mēʾên hᵃpugôt*) is, moreover, taken by the Versions as giving either a reason for the distress (e.g. Syr.'s 'because there is no alleviation', cf. also Vulg.) or its consequence (LXX's 'so that there shall be no rest'). While both these are grammatically possible, the close parallel in 2:18c (Heb. *ʾal-tittᵉnî pûgat lāk ʾal-tiddōm bat-ʿênēk*, 'give yourself no rest, your eyes no respite') suggests that it is *RSV* and other modern English translations (excluding *NEB*, which unnecessarily and without any support emends the text here and in vv. 50–51) which are on the right lines here.

until the LORD from heaven looks down and sees: the hope that God will 'see' (Heb. *rāʾāh*) the situation in which Israel finds itself is frequently expressed, of course, in chapters 1 (vv. 9, 11, 20) and 2 (v. 20).

my eyes cause me grief at the fate of all the maidens of my city: lit. 'my eye deals severely with my soul because of all the daughters of my city'. The verb (Heb. *ʿll*) is found also in 1:12b, 22a, b, and 2:20a. MT is often pronounced unintelligible (e.g. Hillers, 59), which it clearly is not. The thought is either that the eyes have become sore as a result of weeping (Syr., *JB*), or that the eyes, as the medium by which the man gains knowledge of the terrible events happening around him (the 'daughters' of the **city** are probably the 'maidens' of 1:4, 18, 2:10, 21, less likely, as Reʾemi, 112–13, and others have suggested, the towns surrounding Jerusalem), are a source of emotional pain to him (*RSV, NIV*).

52–54. From this point until the end of the poem the speaker returns once again to explore his own individual situation. As was stated in the introduction to the chapter, the perfect verbs of vv. 52–61 are not for the most part best understood as they are in *RSV*. In v. 54a the perfect is most satisfactorily translated as 'has closed', reflecting present distress; in v. 55 a present tense is best ('I call on thy name'); and in vv. 56–61 the perfects are 'precative', and are best rendered as imperatives (e.g. 'hear my plea', v. 56a). 'The man' is still in the same situation as he was in vv. 1–20, and he pleads with God to deliver him. Translations reflecting this overview of the section will appear, where there is divergence from the *RSV* text, in brackets alongside this text below, and the comments will relate to these translations rather than to *RSV*.

I have been hunted like a bird by those who were my enemies without cause: the hunting metaphor appears once more, linking the speaker's individual experience with that of the people as a whole (cf. v. 47, 1:13). The **enemies** had no justification for their action, and are therefore, the verse implies, to be condemned. The idea that Israel's foes were accountable for their actions, even when they were being used as 'the rod of God's wrath', is parallelled elsewhere in the *OT* (e.g. Isa. 10:5–19).

they flung me alive into the pit and cast stones on me: *RSV* (cf. also *NEB*) takes the first part of the line to be a description of how the speaker came to be in **the pit** (he was thrown in) and the state in which he was when this occurred (he was **alive**). It thereby implies that the imagery has changed from that of the hunt to that of human imprisonment. The Heb., however, does not itself say how the author came to be in **the pit**, but simply refers to his presence there and the life-threatening nature of his imprisonment in it. A much better translation is that of *NIV*: 'they tried to end my life in a pit' (cf. v. 58, which refers back to the *ḥayyâ*, 'my life', of this verse in a plea that God would save the speaker from his plight). This translation makes clear that it is possible to understand this line as drawing its imagery, not from human imprisonment, but from the capture of an animal (through its falling into a **pit**) and its subsequent death by stoning (so, for example, Kaiser, 357). Whether one fully agrees with Kaiser and others on this point will depend on the way in which Heb. *'eben*, 'stone', in the second part of the line is understood. This could be taken as a collective noun, and therefore rendered as in *RSV* (cf. also Syr., *JB*, *NIV*), or as a true singular (so LXX, Vulg., *NEB*), the idea being that the hole was sealed to prevent escape. Whatever is the case, it is clear that more is indicated by the use of **pit** (Heb. *bôr*) here than simply a place of imprisonment. The word frequently appears elsewhere in Heb. literature as the abode of the dead, the place into which those praying to God are afraid of entering, in whose power they feel themselves already to be, or from which they have been rescued (e.g. Ps. 30:3 [MT 30:4]; 143:7). By reference to it here the speaker emphasizes the direness of his situation.

water closed over my head; I said, 'I am lost' (water has closed over my head; I said, 'I am lost'): another metaphor which expresses extreme distress is that of submersion in water (e.g. Ps. 42:7 [MT 42:8]; 69:1-2 [MT 69:2-3]; 124:4-5). The speaker feels himself to be as good as dead.

55-57. I called on thy name, O LORD, from the depths of the pit (I call on thy name, O LORD, from the depths of the pit): as D. Michel, *Tempora und Satzstellung in den Psalmen*, (AET 1; Bonn, 1960), 79-81, long ago demonstrated, the perfect of Heb. *qārā'* in appeals to God in the Psalms must often be translated as a present tense, as in the laments Ps. 17:6, 88:9 [MT 88:10], 119:145-146, 130:1, 141:1. There can be little doubt that it is also best translated thus here. In the midst of his current distress in the pit, the speaker cries out for God's help.

thou didst hear my plea, 'Do not close thine ear to my cry for help!' (hear my plea; do not close thine ear to my cry for help!): most attempts to read at least the first part of Lam. 3:52-66 as referring to past suffering and relief (see the introduction to this chapter) have agreed with *RSV* in taking v. 56b as containing the content of a past plea to God. This is not impossible. There is, however, no parallel to such a construction elsewhere in the *OT*. We do occasionally get a reference back to what the petitioner said or thought before prayer began, analogous to what we find in v. 54 (cf. Ps. 31:22 [MT 31:23]). In no other address to God in the *OT*, however, is a statement that he has heard (*sm⁽*) a petition followed by a citation of that petition. If such a reading is accepted, then, we are dealing here with a unique form. There are, on the other hand, many parallels to pleas to God in the present in which verbal or nominal forms from *'zn* are used (e.g. Ps. 10:17, 71:2, 86:1, 130:2, 141:1, 143:1); and the other imperatives in the section—v. 59, if original (see below), and v. 63—both express pleas in the present of this kind. V. 59, indeed, provides a direct parallel (perfect followed by imperative). On balance, then, it would seem rather better to interpret v. 56b also as expressing a plea in the present. If the perfect in 56a were to be understood as a simple past, a translation of v. 56 along the lines of *NEB* would then have to be accepted ('thou heardest my voice; do not turn a deaf ear when I cry, 'Come to my relief'), distinguishing thereby between a past oppression and deliverance from enemies on the one hand, and a present oppression with future deliverance on the other. The sense of the verse would then be: 'you answered my prayer when I was in distress before: please do not ignore my plea for relief on this occasion'. The difficulty of so distinguishing between two situations of oppression has, however, been discussed above (see the introduction to this chapter). It is preferable to take the perfect verb rather as precative: 'hear **my plea: do not close thine ear to my cry for help!**' As Hillers, 59, points out, Ps. 130:1–2 ('Out of the depths I cry to thee, O LORD! Lord, hear my voice! Let thy ears be attentive . . .') provides a particularly good parallel to the progress of thought here. The situation is the same as in v. 44: God has not yet responded to the prayers of his people. **Do not close thine ear** is thus part of the current plea, rather than the content of some past plea which is not recorded elsewhere in the chapter.

   Scholars have often argued that one of the last two words of the line in MT (Heb. *l^{e}rawḥātî l^{e}šaw'ātî*) is a gloss. Of the two, the latter is perhaps the more expected in the context, and is favoured by (among others) Brandscheidt, *Gotteszorn und Menschenleid*, 28. *šaw'āh* appears elsewhere several times, as here, in the context of appeals to God in conjunction with the verb *šāma'*, 'to hear' (note particularly Ps. 18:6 [MT 18:7] and 102:1–2 [MT 102:2–3], where it also appears in conjunction with *qārā'*, 'to call'; and Ps. 40:1 [MT 40:2], with its reference to the 'pit' in the following verse). *r^{e}wāḥāh* (which *RSV* does not translate), on the other hand, otherwise appears only in Exod. 8:15 [MT 8:11], where it seems to have the meaning 'relief, respite'. Commentators such as Kraus, 53, and Kaiser, 346, make a virtue of this, suggesting that *šaw'āh*

has been added to explain the rarer word. There is, however, no
evidence from the Versions that there was ever a Heb. text less
full than the one now available to us: *JB*'s footnote citing the LXX
in favour of a shorter text is misleading, since LXX simply divides
vv. 56–57 slightly differently. Moreover, MT may be translated
quite satisfactorily as it stands, either as: 'Do not close thine ear,
for my relief (i.e. that I may be relieved), to my cry for help'; or,
taking our cue from the root *rwḥ*, 'to breathe', and interpreting
rᵉwāḥāh as 'gasping' (cf. Vulg.) or 'cry', as: 'Do not close thine
ear to my gasping, to my cry for help'. LXX and Syr. both have
a reference to salvation at this point, suggesting that they interpreted
lᵉšawʿātî in the light of, or perhaps read a slightly different word
derived from, the root *yšʿ*, rather than thinking of the root *swʿ*.

**Thou didst come near when I called on thee; thou didst say,
'Do not fear!'** (Come near when I call on thee; tell me not to be
afraid!): in Ps. 69:18 [MT 69:19] God is likewise requested to come
near to one in deep distress; to one, indeed, who describes his
situation in terms very similar to our speaker here (cf. Ps. 69:1–3,
14–15).

**58–60. Thou hast taken up my cause, O Lord, thou hast
redeemed my life** (Take up my cause, O Lord, redeem my life!):
God is also requested to 'take up' the petitioner's cause in such
texts as Ps. 43:1 and 119:154, in the latter of which he is also asked
to 'redeem' him (Heb. *gāʾal*: cf. also Jer. 50:34, with its description
of God as 'Redeemer'). There is a connection here and in the next
two verses with vv. 34–36, where the objector questioned whether
God *could* 'see' that the speaker was being denied his rights by his
enemies (cf. *rîb* in v. 36), whether he had any control over the
situation. In this stanza the speaker requests God that he *would*
'see' (cf. vv. 59–60) and act to redress injustice. The reference to
the speaker's **life** points us back to v. 53, where it was said that
the enemies 'tried to end my life in a pit'.

**Thou hast seen the wrong done to me, O LORD; judge thou
my cause** (See the wrong done to me, O LORD; judge thou my
cause!): the speaker has said in v. 49–50 that he will not stop
weeping until God 'sees' the situation. Vv. 59–60 are best taken

as indicating that this state of affairs has not changed: they are pleas that he *would* see, rather than claims that he *has* seen. He is to see the **wrong done** to the speaker, the **vengeance** which his enemies have wrought on him, and all the plans (*RSV*'s **devices**) which they have made against him, and he is to **judge** his **cause** favourably (cf. *NIV*'s 'Uphold my cause'). LXX and Syr. have a perfect in v. 59b instead of MT's imperative, though on our interpretation of the perfects in this section this makes no difference to the sense.

61–63. More details of the persecution being endured at the hands of the enemies are given, picking up from the reference to their 'plans' in v. 60, whose second part is repeated almost exactly in v. 61: **Thou has heard their taunts, O LORD, all their devices against me** (Hear their taunts, O LORD, all their devices against me). The sufferer is often characterized as being the subject of **taunts** in the Psalms (e.g. Ps. 69:9 [MT 69:10], 79:4) and elsewhere, and we have an earlier reference to this in v. 30 of this chapter. The **lips** of v. 62 stand for that which they utter, perhaps their 'whispers' (cf. *NEB, NIV*) or simply 'words', while the plotting is going on. This they do **all the day long**, whether **sitting** (or 'lying down') or **rising** (i.e. whatever they are doing, cf. Dt. 6:7). There is no respite from their jibes. The speaker is **the burden** (i.e. the subject) **of their songs** at all times (cf. v. 14: for a discussion of LXX and Syr. in v. 63, neither of whose texts fits the context as well as MT, see Albrektson, *Studies*, 168–169).

64–66. The verbs of these final three verses of the chapter are all imperfects, either expressing confidence that God *will* eventually deal with the enemies (*RSV*) or, more probably, continuing the pattern of vv. 56–61, asking that he *would* do so (*JB, NEB, NIV*). Rudolph, 236–237, has attempted to argue that in fact they refer to the past, noting that the imperfect verb *tiqrāʾ* in 2:22 does so, and that both it and the verbs in 3:64–66 can be explained by the need of the author to keep to the acrostic structure and begin his stanza/lines with the Heb. letter *t*. He believes that all of vv. 52–66 refer to a past experience of suffering. The imperative of v. 63 clearly indicates, however, that the end of the third poem, like that of the first, looks to the future, and Rudolph's emendation of this verb, as he himself freely admits (p. 233), has no textual support whatsoever.

Most of the stanza is clear enough. God is to bring on the wicked what they deserve because of their actions (to **requite** them, Heb. *hēšîb g^emûl* cf. Ps. 28:4), to **pursue them** (as he had 'pursued' his own people, v. 43) and **destroy them from under** God's heaven. V. 65 is more difficult, however. Its first part seems to refer (*NEB* differs on this point) to some experience which God will lead them to have, though since Heb. *m^eginnāh* (*RSV*'s **dullness**) occurs only here in the *OT* we cannot be sure what is meant. It is most often understood as a hard covering (cf. Heb. *māgēn*, 'shield', with which LXX and Vulg. also apparently connected the word), *m^eginnat-lēb* then best being taken as referring to the condition known as 'hardness of heart' (cf. *JB*; Kaiser, 346) which elsewhere in the *OT* precedes God's judgement (e.g. Exod. 7:1 ff.). Syr. (cf. *AV*) understood the phrase to refer to sorrow, which also fits the context well (cf. Hillers, 65). Some modern commentators (e.g. Rudolph, 233–234; Kraus, 68) have interpreted it as meaning 'blindness', citing such passages as 2 Kg. 6:18; and others (Gordis, 187–188) as 'madness'. The noun of the second part of the verse, Heb. *ta^ʾlāh*, is also unique to this verse, though it is clearer that it should indeed be translated **curse** with *RSV* (*NEB*'s rendering is very weak here). The Versions all seem to presuppose a Heb. *t^{eʾ}ālāh*, 'weariness, hardship' here, indicating an early confusion in the text as to the order of the consonants ʾ and *l*. Since both texts make good sense, it is difficult to choose between them as to originality.

IN THE STREETS 4:1–22

As in the first three poems, two voices are found in chapter 4. The narrator appears in vv. 1–16, 21–22; and the people of Zion in vv. 17–20. In other respects, however, the fourth poem is quite different from these. It is considerably shorter, each stanza being divided into two rather than three lines; there is no prayer to God,

who is referred to only in the third person; and it ends on a note
of assurance (v. 22a). When read after chapters 1–3, then, it gives
the impression both that the outpouring of words in those chapters
has left the sufferers now with less to say, and, at least in the case
of the narrator, that there is a degree of confidence that their
previous prayers have been heard and are shortly to be answered.
Both voices content themselves simply with description of the
suffering which has been undergone 'in the streets' (Heb. *baḥûṣôt*,
a keynote of this poem: vv. 5, 8, 14, cf. also vv. 1 and 18) in
the wake of the fall of the city. The people express disillusionment
with those who could not save them from their fate, whether those
outside (v. 17) or inside the community (v. 20). The narrator's
main concern is with the suffering of the children, though he is
also concerned once again with what he understands to be the cause
of the tragedy—the sin of the people, particularly of their religious
leaders (v. 13). He is once again more intent than the people on
explanation rather than merely complaint. The closing note of
certainty (v. 22a) as to Zion's bright future is most remarkable
to the reader who has read this far in the book. It is but an
interlude, however, a point of calm in the midst of the storm. The
fifth poem will find us once again in the midst of questions and
doubts.

For a general discussion of the historical circumstances in which
this fourth lament might have been written, see 'Author, Date and
Place of Composition' in the Introduction.

*

**1–2. How the gold has grown dim, how the pure gold is
changed:** Hillers, 78–79, objects to MT here because gold does
not tarnish or grow dark in any striking way; because figurative
language involving gold in the *OT* never otherwise makes reference
to the colour and brightness of gold, but only to its value; and
because the imagery of tarnished gold does not fit well with what
follows in the next line and in v. 2. There the imagery is of precious
or sacred things (or people) now regarded with disdain. He therefore

suggests emendations. The Versions do differ in the detail of the line. Syr. renders the first verb as 'rejected' and takes Heb. *ketem* (*RSV*'s second **gold**) as 'dye', no doubt relating the noun (like Vulg.) to the root *ktm*, 'to be stained' (Jer. 2:22); while LXX, as elsewhere (cf. Albrektson, *Studies*, 173), renders *ketem* loosely, offering 'silver'. They do not support a different understanding of the line as a whole, and it must be asked whether Hillers' objections to MT are very compelling. We are probably to take the line with what follows in v. 1b. The gold has lost its lustre because, like the **stones**, it has been lying **scattered at the head of every street**, or more colloquially, 'at every street corner' (*NEB*). The reference to its change in appearance would not then be inconsistent with the reference to its value in v. 2, if both verses do indeed refer to the same thing. **Holy stones** (Heb. *ʾabnê-qōdeš*) has sometimes been taken (Vulg., *NEB*) as referring to the stones of the Temple, while others have thought that the allusion is to Temple treasure. V. 2 and the following verses, where all the emphasis is upon people, suggest, however, that both the gold and the stones are figures for the inhabitants of Zion. If the translation **holy** is correct, then the thought is specifically of the status of these people as God's people. It is also possible, however, to render *ʾabnê-qōdeš* simply as 'jewels, gems' (so J. A. Emerton, 'The Meaning of *ʾabnê-qōdeš* in Lamentations 4:1', *ZAW* 79 (1967) 233–236), removing all mention of holiness. *NIV* combines both thoughts with its 'sacred gems'. The **sons of Zion**, once regarded as **precious**, are now **reckoned as earthen pots**. The high esteem in which they were held is no more.

3–4. What is the reason for this change in attitude? A once great and prosperous people has been reduced to a starving remnant (vv. 3–10), driven to inhuman behaviour (vv. 3–4, 10). The first to be described (if they are indeed first of a number of groups: see below) are the children, both those still nursing—I Sam. 1:21 ff. suggests that children were breast-fed for a considerably longer time than is usual in modern Western society—and others. They are desperate for sustenance, but their parents are unwilling or unable to provide it. The contrast around which v. 3 is built in

MT is between the behaviour of two desert animals, and it depends upon the negative associations which these animals apparently had in the Hebrew mind. The first is the jackal (Heb. *tan*: LXX, followed by *NEB* with 'whales', seems to have read the noun here as *tannîn*, 'serpent, dragon, sea-monster', which certainly does not fit the context so well). **Even the jackals**, associated in the *OT* with destruction and desolation (e.g. Jer. 9:11 [MT 9:10]), feed their young. The people of Jerusalem (**the daughter of my people**, cf. the comment on 1:6: LXX, followed by *JB, NEB*, has 'daughters', making it clearer that only the women are in mind), however, are more like the *y^eēnîm*, perhaps **ostriches**, though this is disputed. There are certainly aspects of the behaviour of **ostriches** which might have resulted in their gaining a reputation among the ancients for cruelty towards offspring. Under certain environmental conditions, for example, the family group may break up when the chicks are only a few weeks old, the adults renewing sexual activity and becoming highly aggressive towards all juveniles. Chicks fledged in small numbers outside the breeding season are frequently treated as outcasts and live solitarily (cf. S. Cramp (ed.), *Handbook of the Birds of Europe, The Middle East and North Africa: The Birds of the Western Palearctic*, vol. 1, Oxford, 1977, pp. 37–41). The theme of maternal abandonment is, of course, picked up in vv. 4–5.

5. It is not quite clear whether in this verse attention has turned to the fate of the nobility as a whole, or whether it is only children from a privileged background who are in view. Nor is it clear that *RSV* is right to interpret the verse as speaking of death. The main verb of the first line is Heb. *šmm*, which is, as was noted in the discussion of 1:4, ambiguous (cf. also 1:13, 16; 3:11). It may refer either to the circumstances or to the attitude of the subject (**Those who feasted on dainties** or 'delicacies', cf. *NIV*), and is best rendered here either as 'destitute' (*NIV*) or 'desolate' (*NEB*)/'appalled'. It is very doubtful whether it can bear the meaning **perish**. 'Destitute' is perhaps to be preferred, since the second line certainly alludes to a change in circumstances. **those who were brought up in purple** now embrace (*RSV*'s **lie on** is a very weak rendering of Heb. *ḥibbᵉqû*) **ash heaps** or 'rubbish heaps' (*JB*). In view of I Sam. 2:8 and Job 24:8, this is best taken as describing where they now live (with the poor and needy) rather than where they have died. Whereas once they lived a life of luxury (**purple** or scarlet clothing was traditionally associated with wealth, cf. Hillers, 88), now they exist on the margins of society with those who have nothing. The disaster has touched even those who would normally be protected from social ills.

6. For the chastisement of the daughter of my people has been greater than the punishment of Sodom, which was overthrown in a moment: both the *sin* of **Sodom** and the extraordinary **punishment** which fell upon that city, which was destroyed in a moment by God (cf. Gen. 18–19), are frequently cited in the *OT* literature (e.g. Ezek. 16:46–58; Am. 4:11). Either may be in view here, since Heb. *ᶜᵃwōn* and *ḥaṭṭāʾt* elsewhere in the *OT* (cf. I Sam. 28:10; Zech. 14:19) refer both to **chastisement** or **punishment** for sin and (more commonly) to sin itself. The suggestion might be that Jerusalem's behaviour was worse than that of **Sodom** (*JB*), and that this is why she endured the prolonged suffering just illustrated in vv. 3–5 rather than being dispatched quickly. Alternatively, the contrast may simply be between the respective fates of the cities. What is clear is that sudden death is regarded as much to be preferred to the slow and painful demise of the starving, a thought which appears again in v. 9.

no hand being laid on it: there is much dispute as to the precise derivation of the verb *ḥālû* in MT's *wᵉlōʾ-ḥālû bāh yādāyim*, and consequently some difference of opinion about the meaning of this sentence. *RSV* assumes that the allusion is to the lack of human mediation in the case of Sodom's downfall: the action of God was direct and miraculous. The verb *ḥûl* does have the connotation 'turn against, fall upon' in 2 Sam. 3:29, Jer. 23:19 = 30:23, and Hos. 11:6 (so Albrektson, *Studies*, 179–80); and McDaniel, 'Studies', 45–48, draws attention to places in the War Scroll from Qumran where a *ḥl* appears, sometimes with *yad*, 'hand', meaning 'to attack'. *NIV* takes *ḥûl* in a different sense, as meaning 'to turn towards', and translates 'without a hand turned to help her'. *JB* and *NEB* both refer to the wringing of hands, perhaps deriving *ḥālû* from *ḥûl*, which can mean 'to twist', perhaps (like LXX and Syr.) from *ḥālāh*, 'to become weak, sick' ('hands did not become weary in her', thus 'no one wrung his hands'). *JB* interprets this as meaning that there was no time for any expression of distress, while *NEB* is less specific, and could be taken as implying that no sadness was felt by others at Sodom's downfall. With reference to *ḥālāh*, we might also render the sentence: 'hands did not grow weak in her', i.e. her occupants did not have to endure a crippling famine. There is very little to choose between these different suggestions, which do not by any means represent an exhaustive list of the possibilities. The hands probably belong to humans rather than to God (*contra* Dahood, 'Readings', 190), but nothing is clear beyond this.

7-8. The subject of these two verses are the *nᵉzîrîm*, 'those consecrated, set apart'. *RSV* renders this as **princes** (cf. *NEB*'s 'crowned princes', *NIV*'s 'princes': *JB*'s 'young men' rests upon an unsupported emendation), though this translation is perhaps a little too precise (cf. the comments on *śār* in 1:6, 2:9): better 'those of high rank'. If this interpretation is correct, then the thought is similar to that in v. 5: even the nobility have suffered. It is again not clear, however, whether it is only the very young or the nobility more generally who are in the author's mind. *nᵉzîrîm* could also be taken in a religious sense (cf. the Versions, *AV*), and translated 'Nazarites', those dedicated to God by a vow involving abstinence from certain things (cf. Am. 2:11-12). In this case the thought is that the disaster has touched even those most committed to God's cause. The general thrust of the verses is clear enough, then, even if the precise identity of the sufferers is veiled by the language. None has escaped the wrath which has been unleashed against the city.

The consequences of the suffering of the *nᵉzîrîm* are plainly and vividly described. Their bodies (literally 'bones', Heb. *ᶜeṣem* standing for the whole person as in Prov. 16:24) were once beautiful, like **snow, milk, coral** (or perhaps 'rubies', *NIV*: the meaning of Heb. *pᵉnînîm* is not certain) and **sapphire** (or 'lapis lazuli', *NEB*). Now they have changed so much, as a result of the famine, that **they are not recognized in the streets**. Their faces are **blacker**

than soot and **their skin** has dried and **shrivelled**. The only difficulty here is with the phrase *sappîr gizrātām* at the end of v. 7. Heb. *gizrāh* only otherwise appears in the *OT* in Ezek. 41:12–15, 42:1, 10, 13, of the yard adjoining the temple. These occurrences are plainly of little help to us here. The verb with which the noun is usually associated is *gāzar*, 'to cut, divide'. *RSV*'s **beauty of their form** represents a common attempt to understand the noun in the light of this verb, taking the cutting or carving to be that which produces a beautiful object (cf. also Gottwald, *Studies*, 16: more generally, *JB, NIV*). *NEB* prefers to takes its cue from Symm. and an Arabic root *gzr*, translating 'their limbs' (cf. also Albrektson, *Studies*, 182; Kaiser, 360). These translations assume that there is no significance in the fact that **sapphire** and lapis lazuli are blue, even though in the first part of v. 7b something is made of the fact that rubies are, and **coral** can be, red. Other scholars have attempted to render *gizrātām* with blueness in mind. A good case can be made for the translation 'their hair'. Hair is, of course, something which may be cut (cf. Heb. *gāzar*), and there is abundant evidence (cf. Hillers, 81) that lapis lazuli was used in the Ancient Near East to represent hair. If this is right, Ca. 5:10–11, where a description of the body as 'radiant' (Heb. *ṣaḥ*, the same root as in *ṣaḥû*, **whiter**) and ruddy (Heb. *ʾādôm*, the same root as *ʾādᵉmû* here) is followed by a description of the hair, gives a good parallel to the train of thought here. Of course, if the reference in v. 7 is to Nazirites, an allusion to hair at this juncture is even more understandable (cf. Jg. 13:5, 16:17).

9. Happier were the victims of the sword than the victims of hunger: the thought is not, of course, that they were more joyful, but that they were 'more fortunate' (*NEB*, cf. also *NIV*), because their end was immediate. The second line, lit. 'who flowed away (Heb. *zûb*, often used of the flow of blood, e.g. Lev. 15:25), pierced through (Heb. *dāqar*), for lack of (or perhaps 'far from', cf. Albrektson, *Studies*, 184) food from the field', may be understood in two ways. *RSV* renders it **who pined away, stricken by want of the fruits of the field**. If this understanding of the line is correct, we have here a clever continuation of the imagery of 'slaying by the sword' in the first line: the 'wounds' of the hungry could only be healed by eating, and this they were unable to do. Alternatively, though this requires us to supply the verb from the first line, we might understand the verbs *zûb* and *dāqar* as referring literally to **the victims of the sword**: 'they whose blood flowed, being stabbed, than those who perished for lack of the fruits of the field' (Gordis, 190–191; similarly Hillers, 76). Although objection has often been taken to MT at this point (e.g. by Robinson, 'Notes', 259), there is no real difficulty here, and the Versions do not provide any basis for reconstructing a different text.

10. The description of the famine comes to a fitting climax with the information that **The hands of compassionate women have boiled their own children; they became their food**. Gordis, 191, manages to find an allusion to an Akkadian vampire in Heb. *lᵉbārôt*, **food**, translating 'they became vampires to them'. The context in which *lᵉbārôt* appears here, however, and the fact that the root *brh* appears elswhere in the *OT* in references to **food** (e.g. 2 Sam. 13:5, 7, 10), indicates that we are on safer (if not such interesting) ground if we retain the more mundane translation. That it was the nature of these women to be **compassionate** simply brings home the horror of it all, for it is when evil appears in such close proximity to good that it is most shocking. The phrase **the destruction of the daughter of my people** (Heb. *šeber bat–'ammî*) is also found in 2:11 and 3:48, occurring otherwise in the *OT* only in Jer. 8:11, 21.

11. From v. 11 on, the effects of famine fade from view, and other aspects of the disaster are touched upon. The central theme is that the catastrophe represents the punishment of God for sin; and it is this theme which we find clearly expressed in this verse. **The LORD gave full vent to his wrath**, to his **hot anger**, which, as often in the *OT* (e.g. 2:3–4), is characterised as **fire**. This **fire** is said to have **consumed** Zion's **foundations**, a statement which, since stone **foundations** do not burn, should warn us against the temptation (sometimes not resisted by commentators, e.g. Kraus, 78) to regard either the **fire** or the **foundations** as literal. The point is simply that God's anger had a devastating effect.

12. It is, of course, extremely unlikely that **Jerusalem** was very much in the thoughts of **The kings of the earth or the inhabitants of the world** in general, much less that they subscribed to a belief in the city's inviolability. This belief does seem to have been widely shared by the population of Judaea, however, both in the pre-exilic and post-exilic periods, and since Zion was the centre of their universe, it often came to be described in cosmic terms of the kind used here (cf., for example, Ps. 48:1-6 [MT 48:2-7]). Whether the author really believed that these others shared this view of Zion, or whether he is simply using exalted language in order to stress the enormity of what has happened, cannot be known.

13. This was for the sins of her prophets and the iniquities of her priests: although it is possible that v. 13 belongs with v. 12 ('. . . that foe or enemy could enter the gates of Jerusalem because of **the sins** . . .'), it is much more likely either that it stands alone, as in *RSV* (cf. *JB, NEB, NIV*), or (more likely in view of the exegesis of vv. 14-15 which follows below) that it belongs with v. 14 ('Because of **the sins** . . . they wandered blind . . .': so *AV*). **The prophets and the priests** are accused of shedding **the blood of the righteous**. This might simply mean that by failing in their duty to give religious leadership to the people as a whole, and thus precipitating the catastrophe, they are effectively guilty of the murder of those who were blameless. The interpretation of vv. 14-15 which is accepted below demands, however, that a more specific charge is in the author's mind here: that innocent **blood** was spilled in the city *prior* to the events now being described. Whether they are envisaged as personally responsible for murderous acts, or only generally responsible in their capacity as leaders, is not clear.

14-15. Another problem of identification arises here: who are the **They** of these verses who are **defiled with blood** and pronounced **Unclean!**? MT does not make this clear, describing them only as the **blind**. This might refer either to the prophets and/or priests of v. 13a (thus the majority of commentators, cf. Mic. 3:5-7)—those who should see visions are actually sightless—or to the people as a whole (thus Hillers, 90). Blindness could be a metaphor either for their distress (cf. Dt. 28:29; Isa. 59:10; Zeph.

1:17) or for their lack of moral sense in the absence of any guidance from above (cf. Isa. 42:18–20). It is not so easily understood only of the righteous of v. 13b (Kraus, 79–80), given what follows in v. 15. The Versions further complicate matters, LXX reading 'watchmen', Syr. 'nobles', in place of MT's **blind**. The broader context of the verses, however, seems to favour the view that it *is* the people as a whole who are described here. The 'them' of v. 16a, which is most naturally taken as referring to the same group as the **They** here, must surely refer to the community in general which speaks in vv. 17–20. Moreover, v. 18 of this speech seems to have vv. 14–15 in mind (see below). The thought is, then, that the entire community has become **defiled** as a result of the actions or inaction of the religious leaders. They have either participated in murderous acts or have become guilty by association. The same idea, that the shedding of innocent **blood** defiles the land and its people, is found in Ezek. 22:1–5 and Ps. 106:37–39. In both passages a connection is made with idolatry, and it seems probable, given the reference to priests and prophets in the previous verse, that it is crimes specifically connected with religious observance which the author has in mind here.

The imagery of vv. 14b–15 has as its background ancient taboos about cleanness and uncleanness, reflected in such biblical books as Leviticus. In particular, it reflects the treatment meted out to those suffering from leprosy (cf. Lev. 13:45–46). Such unfortunates were required to live apart from the rest of the community and to cry **Unclean!** in order to warn others of their presence. This much is clear. There has been much disagreement, however, about the precise interpretation of the detail here. Some of this disagreement has arisen because of differences of opinion as to whether MT's text in v. 15 is of the correct length. Since the lines of this verse are longer than is usual in the remainder of the poem, many scholars have argued that some of the material is not original to it (cf. *JB, NEB*). There is, however, no Versional evidence which might support any attempt to shorten it, and such a procedure will not be adopted here. This being the case, two main difficulties remain in considering vv. 14b–15.

First of all, there is doubt about the meaning of v. 14b, translated by *RSV* as **that none could touch their garments**. Several scholars (e.g. Rudolph, 246, 248–249) have suggested that this line is better rendered 'they touched (Heb. *yigg ʿû*) with their clothes what they should not have touched', and it is this translation which is accepted here, understanding the reference as to the failure of the unclean in their duty to avoid contact with the rest of the community. This elicits a response from those looking on, in terms both of an reaction of disgust (**Unclean!**) and a rebuke (**Touch not!**, Heb. *ʾal–tiggāʿû*).

There is also doubt, secondly, about the meaning of v. 15ba, rendered by *RSV* as **So they became fugitives and wanderers** (Heb. *kî nāṣû gam–nāʿû*). As this translation illustrates, scholars usually take v. 15ba as a reference to the unclean leaving the community. The meaning of *nāṣû* is, however, uncertain. The translations **became fugitives**, 'left' (*JB*), 'hastened away' (*NEB*), 'flee' (*NIV*) cannot be defended on the basis of other *OT* evidence. Moreover, *nāʿû* appears at the beginning of v. 14a (*RSV*'s **They wandered**), where it refers to the activities of the unclean *within* the community and is best translated 'they staggered' (Ps. 107:27). *kî nāṣû gam–nāʿû* might be better taken, then, as an explanation of the decision which follows in v. 15bb: 'because ruin had come upon them, and they had staggered about, **men said among the nations, "They shall stay with us no longer"**. *nāṣû* in this translation is taken as derived from the root *nṣh* which appears in 2 Kg. 19:25 = Isa. 37:26; Jer. 4:7 (rather than the *nṣh* of Exod. 21:22, 'to struggle, quarrel', which is apparently favoured by the Versions), and means 'to fall in ruins'. Albrektson, *Studies*, 190–191, objects to the interpretation of *lāgûr* in v. 15bb as deriving from the verb *gûr*, **stay with**, on the ground that it makes no sense to say that the people of Jerusalem and Judah were immigrants to the land (cf. *gûr*, for example, in Exod. 12:19). He prefers to connect it with *gûr*, 'to stir up strife, quarrel, attack'. This objection misses the point, however, that we are dealing in vv. 14–15 with an extended metaphor. The people of Zion are *pictured* as living in the midst of the community of nations as sojourners, and as becoming unclean in the course of their sojourning. Afraid of becoming contaminated by them as they stagger **through the streets** (which must on this occasion be taken metaphorically), these **nations** decide that they must leave.

16. The LORD himself has scattered them, he will regard them no more: lit. 'The face of the LORD . . .'. If MT is correct, the point is that the actions of the nations just described are to be seen as the action of God himself. They are merely his agents: it is he who **has scattered** his people. LXX, however, interprets Heb. *ḥlqm* as a noun: 'the presence of the LORD was their portion', referring to the situation before they had to leave their dwelling. Whichever is correct, what is clear is that the people are now in disfavour with God as well as men. As the nations have said that 'they shall stay no longer' (Heb. *yôsîpû*), so God has determined to **regard them no more** (Heb. *yôsîp*), to ignore them and their plight.

no honour was shown to the priests, no favour to the elders: lit. 'they did not lift up the faces of the priests, showed no favour to the elders'. The 'they' can hardly be God (*NEB*), and *JB*'s attempt to take it as referring to the people of Judah and Jerusalem is only plausible because it accepts the reading 'prophets' in place of **elders** with a few Gk. mss. and OL. In all likelihood, however, this minority reading has arisen simply under the influence of v. 13. Those who showed **no honour or favour** are much better taken as the nations of the previous verse, the point being that even those of some standing in the community (the **priests** and **elders**) suffered. None was spared (cf. vv. 5, 7–8), everyone was treated in the same way.

17–20. With v. 17 we change from a third person account to a first person account, analogous to what we find in chapters 1 and 2, though here in the plural rather than the singular. It is evident that the speakers are talking again of events prior to the scattering of vv. 15–16, and *NEB*'s translation of vv. 17–19 as if spoken of the present is therefore inappropriate. It has been suggested that it is the narrator of vv. 1–16 who is still addressing us here, the plural verbs and suffixes in this case simply indicating that he is now more explicitly identifying himself with his people (cf. 3:40

ff. for a parallel). It seems more natural, however, to preserve in these verses the distinction which exists elsewhere in the poem (as indeed in chapters 1 and 2) between narrator and sufferers (cf. vv. 1–3, 21–22), taking the 'we' of these verses as strictly identical with the 'they' of vv. 14–16. It would be particularly awkward to take v. 18a, which seems to allude to vv. 14–15, as spoken by this narrator. The view adopted here, then, is that it is the people of Zion who speak in vv. 17–20, the narrator concluding the poem with vv. 21–22.

17. Our eyes failed, ever watching vainly for help; in our watching we watched for a nation which could not save: the only major difficulty in this verse is with Heb. *bᵉṣippîyātēnû*, rendered somewhat clumsily by *RSV* as **in our watching**. A more idiomatic translation along these lines is found in *NEB*: 'We have watched and watched'. The word appears only here in the *OT*, however, and might equally well be translated 'from our watchtower' (Dahood, 'Readings', 192; cf. *JB, NIV*). The identity of the **nation which could not save** is not made explicit. It is usually assumed by commentators (e.g. Hillers, 91; Kaiser, 370) that the author has Egypt in mind. This is a reading into the text from other documents, however (cf. Jer. 37:5–11), in line with the assumptions usually made about the likely historical background of the poem, rather than a reading out of the text itself. The only nation mentioned by name in the poem is, in fact, Edom, which is attacked by the narrator in vv. 21–22. It seems natural to connect vv. 17 and 21–22, the former giving the background for the sudden diatribe of the latter, and the latter supplying the name missing from the former (cf. Targ.). If this is so, MT is better translated here 'a nation which *does/did* not save', implying *unwillingness* rather than merely *inability* on the part of the guilty nation. There is, indeed, nothing in MT which implies inability, though such an interpretation of the second line is very old (cf. Vulg.).

18–19. Men dogged our steps so that we could not walk in our streets: *NEB* finds difficulty with MT's first verb here, but without cause. The imagery, as what follows in vv. 19–20 makes particularly clear, is that of hunting, and the Heb. verb *ṣādû*, **Men dogged**, comes either from a root *ṣwd* or from a root *ṣdh*, both used elsewhere in the *OT* of hunting, lying in wait. If the line in MT is correct (LXX renders the line quite differently: 'We hunted for our little ones that they should not walk . . .'), and the continuation of the metaphor in vv. 19–20 suggests that it is, then the picture is similar to that in vv. 14–15, and v. 18 alludes to these. The people have come into conflict with their persecutors in the **streets** (though here a different Heb. word, *rᵉḥōbōt*, which might also be rendered 'squares', *JB*: cf. 2:11–12). The **streets** need be no more literal here, of course, than they were in v. 14 or the 'pits' are in v. 20. *JB* has been led, like several commentators (e.g. Albrektson, *Studies*, 192–93), into a very improbable rendering of the verb ('Our enemies eyed our steps'), through lack of comprehension of this fact. As in vv. 14–15, what we have here is a *picture* of oppression. The people were like animals being stalked by hunters who were **swifter than the vultures** (or perhaps 'eagles', *JB, NIV*: Heb. *nešer* may refer to either). Wherever they ran, **streets, mountains, wilderness**, there was no escape. They were on the point of capture (cf. 1:6; 3:52–53): **our end drew near; our days were numbered** (better, 'our life had run its full course'); **for** (better, 'yes,') **our end had come**.

20. **The breath of our nostrils, the LORD's anointed, was taken in their pits, he of whom we said, 'Under his shadow we shall live among the nations'**: the chase is over, a capture made **in their pits**. The focus is upon only one prominent individual among the people, however, who must be their ruler: note the use of **shadow** in Isa. 30:2–3, of **the LORD's anointed** in 2 Sam. 1:16, and of **breath of our nostrils** in extra-biblical sources (cf. Hillers, 92). The latter phrase emphasizes the dependence which the people felt upon their ruler. He was as vital to their lives as **breath** itself (cf. Gen. 2:7, 7:22, and *NIV*'s 'our very life breath'). **shadow** is a common metaphor for protection in the *OT* (e.g. Num. 14:9; Jg. 9:15; Ps. 17:8; and *NEB*'s 'safe under his protection'). His loss is a devastating one. Far from enabling the people to live safely among the nations, he himself has been ensnared by them.

21-22. The poem ends with an attack on **Edom** and a promise to **Zion**. **Edom** (also associated with **Uz** in Gen. 36, cf. v. 28) is attacked apparently because she gloats over Zion's fate (**Rejoice and be glad, O daughter of Edom**). The poet's response is to warn her that God will soon **uncover** her **sins** also, and **will punish** her in the light of them. The perfect verbs here in v. 22b (Heb. *pāqad, gillāh*) must, in view of the imperfects in v. 21b, be taken as 'perfects of confidence', expressing assurance that something will happen in the future. The metaphor of **the cup** (Heb. *kôs*) filled with God's wrath is commonly found elsewhere in descriptions of the divine wrath, as is the imagery of drunkenness for its results (e.g. Jer. 25:15–29). Drunkenness and self-exposure are further associated in Gen. 9:21–22 and Hab. 2:15–16. Nakedness of such a kind was, of course, a source of great shame (cf. the comment on 1:8–9, and *NEB*'s rendering here: 'you will expose yourself to shame'). MT in v. 21b is thus much more coherent than LXX ('you shall become drunk and pour forth') or Syr. ('you shall be miserable and exhausted'), and is to be preferred. **Edom** will suffer a reversal of her fortunes which will reduce her to the same shameful state as **Zion** now finds herself in. **Zion**, on the other hand, has a bright future. *RSV* (along with *JB* and *NEB*) translates v. 22a so as to suggest that her **punishment** is already over: **The punishment of your iniquity, O daughter of Zion, is accomplished, he will keep you in exile no longer**. It seems much more likely, however, that the perfect verb *tam* is to be taken in the same way as the perfect verbs in v. 22b. *NIV*'s 'your punishment will end; he will not prolong your exile' is therefore much better. Nevertheless, it is clear that we have here the first and last real note of unfettered hope in the book. In contrast to the marked lack of hope throughout chapters 1 and 2 (contrast especially the end of chapter 1 with the end of chapter 4), and the tortured vacillation between faith and doubt in chapter 3, here at last is a note of assurance. Things *will* in the end get better!

DISGRACE AND DOUBT **5:1-22**

The main theme of the fifth poem, in which only one voice, the collective 'we', speaks, is the shame (v. 1) of all that has happened to the people. A once proud and free people are now economically dependent upon their oppressors (vv. 4, 6). Women have been raped, men of stature humiliated, young men forced to perform demeaning tasks (vv. 11–13). An important sub-theme is that of accusation of God. It is hinted that he has not kept his promises (vv. 2–3, 5) and stated that he has forgotten his people (v. 20). Whether the 'we' of this poem may be understood, in the context of the book as a whole, as including the narrator of the earlier poems is not clear. What is clear, however, is that the hope expressed by him at the end of chapter 4 is not found in chapter 5. The fifth poem, and the book as a whole, ends in questions (v. 20) and doubt (v. 22). Chapter 5 is also different from chapter 4, and indeed the other poems in the book, in other respects. It is much shorter, having only one line in each verse; it is not an acrostic poem, although it is, like the acrostics, built around the number of letters (22) in the Hebrew alphabet; and it consists predominantly of lines whose parts balance each other, rather than in the unbalanced lines (3:2) of the *qînāh* metre. Within the context of the book as a whole, then, it gives the impression that words are beginning to fail in the face of God's lack of response to the people's plight (cf. Shea, 'Structure', who argues that the book is designed on a *qînāh* pattern, a 'pattern which dies away', three longer chapters being followed by two shorter ones). Indeed, the poem hints that the very attempt to impose structure upon the chaos which the disaster has brought is under threat. Structure and content conspire together, then, to provide the book of Lamentations with a very unsettling ending.

The absence of any acrostic structure in the fifth poem has made it possible for it to be asked whether the poem came into being as an entity, or is a composite piece of work. Several scholars have argued that an older, shorter poem lies at the core of chapter 5, and that this poem was subsequently expanded to its present 22 verses. This case has most recently been made by Kaiser, 376–78, and Brunet, 'La cinquième Lamentation', whose main argument is that vv. 7 and 16 are contradictory. This is unconvincing, however. In the first place, Dan. 9:16 shows that the sins of the fathers and the sins of the present generation could both and at the same time be held as contributing to disaster. We cannot assume, then, that v. 7 means to offload the guilt of the present generation on to past generations. Even if this were its intention, secondly, it would not be sufficient evidence that it was written by a different author to v. 16. For change in perspective is a feature of the other poems as well; and such vacillation between different points of view would be no different to that found, for example, in chapter 3. The fifth poem, then, is best understood, like the other four, as an original unity.

For a general discussion of the historical circumstances in which this lament might have been composed, see 'Author, Date and Place of Composition' in the Introduction.

*

1–2. In some Greek and Latin mss., the fifth poem bears the title 'A prayer' or 'a prayer of the prophet Jeremiah', the latter reflecting the tradition that Jeremiah wrote the book (see the Introduction). No such title is found in MT. As elsewhere in the book, and particularly in chapter 1, God is invited to **behold** (Heb. *habbîṭā*, 1:11; 2:20; 3:63) and **see** (Heb. *rᵊʾēh*, 1:9, 11, 20; 2:20) what has **befallen** his people. He is further requested to **remember** it (a request also found in other communal laments, e.g. Ps. 74:18, 22), the emphasis once more being upon the **disgrace** of it all (cf., for example, 1:8–9). A description of suffering follows in vv. 2–18, the people's first complaint being that they have lost their homes: **Our inheritance has been turned over to strangers, our homes to aliens**. The land promised to Israel in ancient times (cf. Heb. *naḥᵃlāh*, **inheritance** in Num. 26:53, Dt. 4:38, for example) is now in the possession of those with no claim to it. This is not to say that the speakers are elsewhere. What follows in the succeeding verses makes it clear that they are not. The emphasis is rather upon the question of who has the power, who controls the resources.

3. We have become orphans, fatherless; our mothers are like

widows: the **mothers** are not actually **widows**, but only **like widows**. The rendering 'are indeed widows', taking the k^e in k^{e}*almānôt* as asseverative (so Gordis, 195; Meek, 35; Kaiser, 374) does not seem to make much sense here. There is, then, no allusion to the loss of the male population in battle (*contra* Fuerst, 257 *et al.*). There may be an allusion to their deportation (cf. 1:1, in the light of which Rudolph, 260, implausibly and with no textual support, emends **mothers and widows** so as to make them singulars), though even this is questionable. It seems much more likely that the whole people is in view (so Hillers, 103), and that the comparison to **orphans** and **widows** is intended to emphasize the vulnerability which they as a whole feel in their new situation. **orphans** and **widows** were widely recognized in the *OT*, as elsewhere in Ancient Near Eastern texts, as among those least able to defend themselves against exploitation, and consequently among those most in need of protection from others, particularly God (cf., for example, Dt. 10:18). It is precisely such protection which the people seek from God here, and this, we may suggest, is the reason for their choice of self-description.

4. We must pay for the water we drink, the wood we get must be bought: *JB*'s rendering is, in the context, slightly better: 'We drink our own water—at a price; we have to pay for what is our own firewood' (cf. also *NEB*). The people are vulnerable precisely because they have no control over their resources. They are entirely dependent upon those who are now in the ascendancy in the land.

5. With a yoke on our necks we are hard driven; we are weary, we are given no rest: *RSV* follows Symm. in adding a reference to **a yoke** here, a not implausible emendation of MT in view of the identity in the consonantal text between *'ōl*, **yokē**, and *'al*, **on**, and one which has been very popular (cf. *JB* and *NEB*; Kraus, 85; Meek, 35–36; Hillers, 97; Kaiser, 374). McDaniel, 'Studies', 50–51, combines this emendation with another on the basis of Syr., taking the final verb (further emended) of v. 4 along with the beginning of v. 5: 'they put our neck to the yoke'. Although this combined reading itself lacks any textual support, it at least has the merit of divorcing the verb *nirdāpnû* (*RSV*'s **we are hard**

driven) from the beginning of the line. *rādap* would be a most curious verb to use in this way, and it is certainly not so used in the remainder of the book, where it is always 'to pursue, persecute' (1:3, 6; 3:43, 66; 4:19). Allusions to weariness and lack of **rest** are also found in some of those contexts (cf. the comments particularly on 1:3, 6, and compare especially *mānôaḥ* in 1:3 with *ḥûnaḥ* here). It seems much more probable, then, that we have throughout the verse, as in those places, the use of hunting imagery, rather than agricultural imagery. MT (which is supported by LXX) is, in fact, quite comprehensible (so, rightly, Albrektson, *Studies*, 197–198), in spite of the protestations of most scholars to the contrary: 'upon our necks we are pursued'. The picture is of close pursuit, the expression analogous to the colloquial English 'they were breathing down our necks'. Indeed, if we take the imagery on this occasion as reflecting the pursuit of animal by predator, rather than that of animal by human hunter, the idea could be that the predator is on the point of making the kill. His teeth are poised above the neck of the unfortunate victim, ready to strike at the jugular. The people of Judah are, naturally, **weary** from their attempts to avoid such unwelcome attentions. Where v. 4 has spoken of *dependence* upon those who now control their destiny, then, v. 5 speaks further of actual persecution. Not content with possession of the resources, these people actively and relentlessly harry the Judaeans, making their life a misery. The mention of lack of **rest**, of course, reminds us, like the mention of 'inheritance' in v. 2, of the theological significance of what has happened. God had promised the Israelites that they *would* have **rest** in the promised land, especially rest from enemies (e.g. Dt. 12:10). It is also, one suspects, intended to remind God of this. As in vv. 2 and 3, there is a hint of the reproach that God has not kept his word.

6. We have given the hand to Egypt, and to Assyria, to get bread enough: Heb. *nātannû yād*, **We have given the hand**, might mean one of two things. It might refer, first, simply to the action of putting out the hand (cf. Gen. 38:28), signifying a request for bread (*JB*; Kaiser, 374). It could refer, secondly, to an act of submission and commitment (Jer. 50:15; Ezek. 17:18; I Chr. 29:24;

2 Chr. 30:8), the purpose of which is **to get bread** (*NEB, NIV*). Many commentators who favour the latter interpretation (e.g. Kraus, 88; Hillers, 98, 104) explain the verse as reflecting upon the past. In days gone by, Judah had made foreign alliances for economic as well as strategic reasons, this representing the sin of the fathers which is mentioned in v. 7. It seems much more natural, however, to associate the reference to the lack of bread with the present difficulties already mentioned in vv. 4–5, and to interpret it, not as indicating flight from this suffering (*contra* Meek, 36; Kaiser, 380, for example), but as describing the struggle to cope with it. V. 9 further alludes to this struggle (see below). The Judaeans who have remained in the land, deprived of resources near at hand, have had to depend upon outside help. Whether we ought to understand this as implying formal agreements with others or not is in the nature of the case unclear. It is also unclear whether **Egypt** and **Assyria** are to be taken literally. The names of Israel's traditional enemies are by no means always used thus in the *OT*, as indeed they are not in the *NT* (cf., for example, the use of Babylon in the Book of Revelation). The use of these names here might, then, simply be a way of drawing attention to the irony of their situation. They are now dependent for survival upon those who were once their enemies. If **Egypt** and **Assyria** are intended literally, on the other hand, then the author might have in mind help from exiled Israelites in these places, since both are mentioned elsewhere in the *OT* as places of exile (e.g. Isa. 27:13). In sum, nothing is clear about the interpretation of this verse!

7. Our fathers sinned, and are no more; and we bear their iniquities: clearer is *NIV*'s 'we bear their punishment'. What has happened is not to be explained simply as bad luck or 'fate': it is rather punishment for sin. The notion that the sins of one generation could be visited on subsequent ones is well-attested in the *OT* (e.g. Exod. 20:5), though it was not thought inconsistent at the same time to believe that personal responsibility formed part of the picture (Dan. 9:16). V. 16 makes clear that the author of this poem himself had no difficulty in holding these two ideas together. Note the clever poetic play on words between vv. 3 and 7, which hinges on the two different senses of 'fatherlessness' in the two verses: **Our fathers . . . are no more**, Heb. *ʾᵃbōtênû . . . ʾênām*, linking up with Heb. *ʾên ʾāb*, 'fatherless'. As the absence of **fathers** in v. 3 left the people to cope with their oppressors alone, so here their absence leaves them to cope with God. Neither inheritance is particularly pleasant.

8. Slaves rule over us; there is none to deliver us from their hand: Heb. *ʿebed*, 'servant, slave', is used of a wide range of people in the *OT*, and not just of household slaves (Gen 39:17). We find it used also of royal officials (I Kg. 1:47), vassal kings (2 Sam. 10:19), and so on—of anyone in a subservient relation to another. Without further information about the people in view here, then, it is impossible to know to what *ʿᵃbādîm* might refer. It might be officials of a foreign power (Targ.; *JB*; Hillers, 105, and many others; cf. v. 2), or Judaean officials, or some other group. We simply cannot tell. It is likely in any case that the language is partly influenced by the desire, evident also in other verses of the chapter, to emphasize what a great reversal of fortune has taken place, and consequently that it should not be pressed. **Slaves** have become rulers, proverbially one of the four worst possible happenings (Prov. 30:21–23). The situation is thus extremely bad, the more so because **there is none to deliver** the people **from their hand**. This expression is, of course, reminiscent of those found, also in the context of oppression, in the book of Judges (e.g. Jg. 2:16, 18; 8:34). There, deliverers were provided. Here, however, they are entirely absent.

9. We get our bread at the peril of our lives, because of the sword in the wilderness: the main difficulty here is the mysterious reference to **the sword in the wilderness** (Heb. *ḥereb hammidbār*). It is not clear whether this is an allusion to attacks or threats by people who live **in the wilderness** (e.g. Kraus, 89; Gottlieb, *Study*, 69–70); a metaphor for the severity of the heat there (similarly Gordis, 195, though he unnecessarily and implausibly introduces a different *ḥereb* which he thinks *means* 'heat'; cf. *NEB*'s 'scorching heat', reading MT's consonants as *ḥōreb* rather than *ḥereb*); or simply for the deadly nature of **the wilderness** in general. The other difficulty is the nature of the relationship between the dangers of the **wilderness** and the obtaining of **bread**. *JB* talks of the 'earning' of **bread**, taking it as food for which daily work is done, and the dangers as a routine aspect of this activity. It seems more likely, however, that the **bread** in question is that of v. 6—the resources from outside upon which the people are forced to depend because of the internal oppression under which they suffer. The verse tells us, then, of the dangers which the fetching of these resources entails.

10. Our skin is hot as an oven with the burning heat of famine: this verse obviously describes the effects of hunger, though how it is best translated in its detail is a matter of dispute. **The skin** of the people is like **an oven**, but in what respect? Uncertainty is already apparent in the Versions. LXX and Syr. both apparently offer two translations of the verb (Heb. *nikmārû*, *RSV*'s **is hot**), 'has become black and blue' and 'has become shrivelled', while Vulg. has 'is burned up, inflamed' and Targ. 'has become darkened'. Of the modern commentators, several (e.g. Kraus, 89) interpret it, as *RSV* does, in terms of heat; others (e.g. Hillers, 95, 98; Dahood, 'Readings', 194) in terms of blackness (cf. *kimrîr*, 'darkness', in Job 3:5); and still others (e.g. Albrektson, *Studies*, 200) in terms of wrinkling or shrinking, thinking of the clay of an oven which is cracked by heat and flakes off. It is difficult with such a rare form to come to any definite conclusion. The verb *kmr* is used elsewhere in the *OT* only three times, always of emotions (Gen. 43:30; 1 Kg. 3:26; Hos. 11:8). There it seems to mean something like 'to stir up, put in a ferment'. The end of the verse, **with the burning heat of famine**, gives us no help. Heb. *zal⁽ᵃ⁾pôt* (*RSV*'s **burning heat**) is itself rare (only Ps. 11:6, 119:53) and is also variously translated by the Versions, Syr. referring to 'exhaustion', LXX and Vulg. to atmospheric turbulence. It is by no means clear that a translation implying heat is necessary (cf., for example, *NEB*'s 'ravages'); and even if we rendered the word thus, it would still be unclear whether actual **heat** (e.g. fever induced by **famine**, *JB*, *NIV*) is in mind or simply the generally oppressive nature of **famine**. In no case would we be any further forward in an attempt to comprehend the precise connection which the author had in mind between the **famine** and the **skin**.

11. Women are ravished in Zion, virgins in the towns of Judah: the difficulties described so far are general and affect the population as a whole. In vv. 11–14, however, the author turns his attention to particular groups within the community and their specific fates. The emphasis is upon their disgrace (cf. v. 1) and humiliation. The verb of this verse itself, indeed, is Heb. *ʿinnāh*, 'to humiliate', a verb often used elsewhere in the *OT* with the precise connotation of 'to rape' (e.g. Gen. 34:2). As is all too often the case in situations of defeat and oppression, this was the particular fate of the **Women** and **virgins**.

12. Princes are hung up by their hands; no respect is shown to the elders: the latter part of the line is clear enough. The leading men of the community are shown **no respect** by their new masters. Many commentators (e.g. Kraus, 89–90) have in addition seen in the phrase **Princes** (cf. the comment in 1:6) **are hung up by their hands** a reference to execution, perhaps by hanging, impalement, or even crucifixion. It is not clear whether Heb. *bᵉyādām* is to be taken as telling us the means by which they were **hung up** or that they were **hung up** 'at their hands' (*JB*), i.e. at the hands of the oppressors (Meek, 37; Hillers, 95). Death is not necessarily implied, however. The 'hanging up' may have been designed simply to humiliate, perhaps to torture, and not necessarily to kill.

13. Young men are compelled to grind at the mill; and boys stagger under loads of wood: Heb. *ṭᵉḥôn* (*RSV*'s **mill**) occurs only here in the *OT*, and the precise sense of the first part of the line is obscure (cf. Albrektson, *Studies*, 201–2). The verb *ṭāḥan*, 'to grind', is, however, well-known, and in view of this and the reference to the gathering of **wood** (lit. '**boys** stumble on account of **wood**') later in the verse there can be little doubt (in spite of LXX's 'weeping' and Vulg.'s reference to sexual abuse) that we have here a reference to the grinding of corn. Both the grinding of corn and the gathering of **wood** were menial tasks which it would have been regarded as humiliating for **Young men** to perform (cf. Exod. 11:5; Jg. 16:21; Isa. 47:2).

14–16. The old men have quit the city gate, the young men

their music: *RSV* unnecessarily obscures the fact that the **old men** (Heb. *z^eqēnîm*) of this verse are identical with the 'elders' of v. 12, as the **young men** are the same as in v. 13. The elders **have quit the city gate**, where they would normally have sat in an official judicial capacity (cf., for example, Dt. 21:18–21, 22:13–19), while the **young men** have ceased **their music**. Where there was once the dignity of age and the joy of youth, now there is only humiliation and disgrace. V. 15 generalizes the themes of 'quitting' (Heb. *šābat*) and joy from v. 14. **The joy of** the people's **hearts has ceased** (Heb. *šābat*), and where there was once **dancing** there is now only **mourning**. They have lost their **crown**, a symbol of glory and honour (Job 19:9) or festivity (Ca. 3:11): both ideas may well be present here. V. 16 closes with recognition of the reason for the calamity: **we have sinned!**.

17–18. For this our heart has become sick, for these things our eyes have grown dim: *RSV*, in common with the other modern English translations and many commentators, takes the fate of **Mount Zion** in v. 18 as the reason for the people's sickness of **heart** and dimness of **eyes** in v. 17. As Hillers, 99–100, rightly points out, however, the plural **these things** is more naturally taken of what precedes in vv. 2–16. It is because of all *these* happenings that **eyes have grown dim**. The verb *ḥāšak*, 'to be or grow dark', is only used elsewhere of **eyes** growing dim in Ps. 69:23 [MT 69:24] and Ec. 12:3, both in the context of loss of vitality or ageing. The events described have sapped the people's vitality, their joy in living. The reference to sickness of **heart** probably alludes in part to the same thing, though the singular **For this**, which most naturally refers back to 'we have sinned' in v. 16b, and the use of the adjective *dāweh*, **sick**, suggests also a moral dimension. *dāweh* also appears in 1:13, where it carries the connotation of impurity (cf. the comment on 1:13). The sense of the line, then, is: 'Because we have sinned, we have become unclean and sick at heart; because of all the calamities which have befallen us, we have lost our vitality, our zest for life'. V. 18 must then be taken as an unconnected statement which brings the complaint of vv. 1–18 to a climax: 'upon **Mount Zion which lies desolate, jackals** (perhaps 'foxes') **prowl**'.

The central calamity to which all the others are connected is what has happened to **Mount Zion**, which is described as devoid of human presence and the abode only of wild animals. Such a fate for cities is often found promised in ancient texts (e.g. Isa. 13:19–22).

19. With v. 19 complaint gives way to petition. Remembrance of events gives way to remembrance of the nature of God, which is the ground of the petition: **But thou, O LORD, dost reign for ever; thy throne endures to all generations** (better, 'from one generation to another, *NEB*). As Meek, 38, puts it: 'Against the changeful fortunes of men the poet sets the strength and stability of God's throne . . .'.

20–21. Why dost thou forget us for ever, why dost thou so long forsake us?: the accusation that God has forgotten his people was implicit in the opening 'remember' of v. 1, but here it is candidly stated. A better rendering of the first part of v. 20 is found in Hillers, 96: 'Why do you never think of us?'. The accusation is followed by a plea: that God would **Restore** his people to himself, giving them back what they had **of old** (cf. 1:7).

22. Or hast thou utterly rejected us? Art thou exceedingly angry with us?: there has been much dispute about the precise manner in which this verse is connected to what precedes. In LXX and Syr., which apparently read at the beginning of the line the Heb. *kî* ('for') found in a few Heb. mss. instead of MT's *kî 'im*, there is only a very general connection: 'for thou hast rejected . . .'. *RSV* is at best very loose in its rendering of MT's *kî 'im* as **Or** and its framing of the line as two questions. *NEB* has some support (e.g. Meek, 38) for its 'For if thou hast utterly rejected us, then great indeed has been thy anger against us', though this does destroy the parallelism of the verse. The position of *kî 'im* at the beginning of the new line certainly tells against its rendering (with R. Gordis, 'The Conclusion of the Book of Lamentations (5:22)', *JBL* 93 (1974) 289–93) as 'even if, although', as in Lam 3:32. Better than these are 'unless you have utterly rejected us and are angry . . .' (*NIV*, cf. *JB*, Rudolph, 257–58) or 'But you have utterly rejected us and are angry . . .' (cf. Vulg.; Albrektson, *Studies*, 205–7; Hillers,

100–1). Whichever rendering is accepted, it is clear (even in LXX and Syr.) that the poem does not have a confident ending, and it is difficult to see how it is that so many commentators (e.g. Streane, 364; Rudolph, 262–263; Kraus, 91) have come to the conclusion that it does. Attention is emphatically drawn in the verse to the ongoing rejection endured by the people and to the ever-present anger of God. There is no certainty that either of these things will come to end, only a plea that they would. In this respect the mood of the fifth poem is consonant with that of the book as a whole, which struggles to find hope, but is only occasionally truly hopeful.

INDEX OF AUTHORS

INDEX OF BIBLICAL REFERENCES